YORDAN KALEV ZHEKOV

ORIGINS AND DEVELOPMENT

OF

THE TWO AEONS CONCEPT

Origins and Development of the Two Aeons Concept

ISBN: 9798831277128

Imprint: Independently published

Although the author made every effort to ensure the information in this book was accurate at the time of publication, the author does not assume and hereby disclaims any liability to any party for any loss, damage, or disruption caused by errors or omissions, whether such errors or omissions result from negligence, accident, or any other cause.

Printed by Kindle Direct Publishing (KDP), North Charleston SC, an Amazon.com Company, USA

TABLE OF CONTENTS

INTRODUCTION

At the turn of the new millennium with the extraordinary technological advances and achievements of mankind in all spheres of life, our attention toward the future has become stronger than ever before. Humanity is looking ahead expecting to grasp what the future will bring to it. At this time, one particular subject is receiving more and more attention. That is the topic of Apocalyptic, the revealing of future events. The 21st century man is more and more preoccupied with thoughts about the future, his own and of the whole world. Thus, if one of the primary concerns of the today's man is the Apocalyptic, how should we as Christians respond to it? And moreover, have we been engaged enough with analyzing the Apocalyptic in relation to Christianity? Finally, does the subject of Apocalyptic deserve such an attention from the New Testament perspective? Those questions are leading to the issue of the place of Apocalyptic in the New Testament. Regarding the use of the Apocalyptic in the New Testament, George E. Ladd concludes:

> All of the major doctrines of New Testament theology find their meaning in Apocalyptic. Apocalyptic, however, does not remain alone - future event. It has taken on a different guise and descended into history in the person, mission, and ministry of Jesus Christ of Nazareth. Also because of what we have already experienced, we are certain that we shall yet experience the day of judgement when our acquittal will be finally pronounced, and when we shall enter into our glorious resurrection bodies. Apocalyptic is thus at the very heart of the Christian faith.[1]

Ladd explicitly states that the Apocalyptic lies at the heart of Christian faith and the body of Christian doctrines. However, if we extend our scope even further in the content of Apocalyptic itself, we would find that one specific doctrine lies at the very heart of the latter. The basic nuances of that

---

[1] George E. Ladd, "New Testament Apocalyptic," *Review and Expositor* 78 (Spring 1981): 208.

doctrine are easily grasped even from the very words of Ladd. This is the concept of the two aeons. Thus, P. Vielhauer states:

> The essential feature of Apocalyptic is its dualism which, in various expressions, dominates its thought-world. Above all, in the doctrine of the Two Ages, in the dualistic time-scheme of world eras (*ho aiōn toutō* and *ho aiōn mellōn*), the entire course of the world is comprehended.[2]

Thus, we would dare to say that the doctrine of the two aeons is very crucial for an understanding of Christian life and theology and even it can be looked on as staying at the very heart of the latter. In this respect James Robert Ross argues that "…one of the most decisive and crucial aspects of the Christian life is that it involves the believer in the life of two ages, or in two radically different realms of kingdoms."[3] Hence, we are placed in front of the important issue from which understanding depends: the proper understanding of Christian theology as a whole. With such an impression we need to overtake seriously the task to analyze and present appropriately the origins and development of the doctrine of the two aeons up till its New Testament usage. We will perform this research through two general steps. First, we will analyze the prophetic and Apocalyptic traditions and their eschatology. And second, we will turn to analysis of the New Testament.

---

[2] P. Vielhauer, "Introduction," in *New Testament Apocrypha*, eds. E Hennecke and W. Schneemelcher, vol.2 (Great Britain: Lutterworth Press, 1965), 588. Also, Arthur J. Ferch, "The Two Aeons and The Messiah in Pseudo-Philo, 4Ezrea, and 2Baruch," *Andrews University Seminary Studies 15* (Autumn 1970): 135, and Leander E. Keck, "Paul and Apocalyptic Theology," *Interpretation: A Journal of Bible and Theology* 38 (July 1984): 234.

[3] James Robert Ross, "Living Between Two Ages," in *Handbook of Biblical Prophecy*, eds. Carl E. Argmerding and W. Ward Gascque (Grand Rapids, Michigan: Baker Book House, 1978), 231.

PART I. ORIGINS AND DEVELOPMENT OF THE TWO AEONS CONCEPT IN PROPHETIC AND APOCALYPTIC TRADITIONS

Our first main analysis will attempt to establish the origins and development of the two aeons concept in Prophetic and Apocalyptic traditions. Thus, we will examine those traditions in general and their eschatology in particular. Furthermore, we will look at the concept through underlining the continuity and discontinuity between their eschatology.

A. PROPHETIC ESCHATOLOGY

In our attempt to assess carefully the prophetic eschatology of Israel in relation to the concept of the two aeons we need to consider closely the exposition of prophetic tradition of Gerhard von Rad. In the first volume of his, *OT Theology: The Theology of Israel's Historical Traditions*, von Rad exposes "the themes of the Hexateuch which are in substance the characteristic 'actions' of Yahweh, whereby Yahweh has decisively intervened in the life of Israel." Applying his main "programmatic statement",[4] von Rad exposes Israel's history as a history of faith in the one who has been acting in behalf of his people. God was acting in behalf of Israel in her past. Those actions of God were reproduced in the form of recitals that carried the religious inheritance of Israel throughout the ages.

---

[4] Von Rad's "programmatic statement" which became the core of his subsequent work appeared in his essay "The Form-Critical Problem of the Hexaeuch." This work has been written in the time when the National Socialistic regime gained positions in Germany. Hence, it should be kept in mind that it absorbed the struggle of the church during this period. The statement of von Rad is based on the recitals of Deut 26:5-9, 6:20-24, and Josh 24:1-13. They, according to von Rad, establish "Israel's earliest and most characteristic theological articulation." Their content, expressed in the form of worship, instructions and narrative, basically presents the formal acts of Yahweh in Israel's history. On the basis of these recitals von Rad's basic view of Israel's theology has emerged. It is "a narrative rendering of what has happened in Israel's past, a narrative that still has decisive, defining power for subsequent generations."

"God's mighty deeds" became the main source of encouragement, trust, and faith of the future generations of Israel in the one, Yahweh, who has proved to be her sovereign God and savior. In this way "God's mighty deeds" have been relevant for each new generation of Israel, and furthermore each generation have received them as normative for its life and made them applicable for its own situation. Thus, von Rad upholds "the historical dynamic of Israel's faith." In, *The Theology of Israel's Prophetic Tradition,* von Rad continues to discuss the transmission and articulation of the recital of "God's mighty deeds" but now through the view of Israel's prophets. The latter continued to use the recital but, in a way, applicable to their time and circumstances, without restricting themselves to the old tradition but even criticizing it.[5]

With this framework of von Rad's understanding of the prophetic messages we need to look at prophetic eschatology in order to conceive the prophetic understanding of the two aeons concept. Hence, at first we will furnish our discussion with the following definition of prophetic eschatology.

> Prophetic eschatology we define as a religious perspective which focuses on the prophetic announcement to the nation of the divine plans for Israel and the world which the prophet has witnessed unfolding in the divine council and which he translates into the terms of plain history, real politics, and human instrumentality; that is, the prophet interprets for the king and the people how the plans of the divine council will be effected within the context of their nation's history and the history of the world.[6]

We can not, however, go further in unfolding the eschatology of the prophets without considering the view of time and history which shaped

---

[5] Walter Brueggemann, *Theology of the Old Testament: Testimony, Dispute, Advocacy* (Minneapolis: Fortress Press, 1997), 16-38.

[6] Paul D. Hanson, *The Dawn of Apocalyptic: The Historical and Sociological Roots of Jewish Apocalyptic Eschatology* (Philadelphia: Fortress Press, 1975), 11.

Part I. Origins and Development of the Two Aeons Concept in Prophetic and Apocalyptic Traditions

their eschatology. This understanding is based on von Rad's idea that the understanding of prophetic eschatology is directly related to the understanding of Israel's ideas about time and history. Hence together with von Rad we will look at the origins of Hebrew thought about history and time and in their light, we will examine the prophetic eschatology.

Von Rad's discussion about Israel's original ideas of history is directly related to the understanding of time by ancient Near-East cultures in general and of Israel in particular. He presents the perspective of time, which the latter had, in the light of our 20th Century view of time. We, the people of 20th Century, have a purely linear view of time. Time viewed as; the past, the one side of the line; the present, the middle of the line; and the future, the other side of the line. The person just picks up events and marks them on the line. This kind of understanding of time as an absolute concept, independent of events is completely strange for Israel. Jewish people viewed time as built by events. For them the events themselves made the time and the time could not exist apart from the events. Moreover our 20th Century view of time is eschatological. We, as a folk, nation or other group of people, view ourselves "as moving towards some ultimate fulfillment."[7] However, this eschatological concept of time was foreign to both Hebrew and Greek people of the ancient world. The Greeks for example viewed time as "cyclical, periodic, always turning back to its beginning once the end has been reached."[8]

> According to Herodotus, the law of time which events obey is not chiliastic, does not press on towards a future, cannot be compared to a stream, nor is in any sense whatsoever eschatological, but it is cyclical, periodic, always turning back to its beginning once the end has been reached. His [Herodotus's] philosophy is … that human affairs run in a cycle…. This mode of viewing events in time… asserts that in, with and

---

[7] Gerhard von Rad, *Old Testament Theology*, vol. 2 (*The Theology of Israel's Prophetic Traditions*. New York: Harper and Row, Publishers, 1965), 101.

[8] Ibid.

under the causal nexus visible and comprehensible to man there is one which is invisible, and which shows itself covertly in, and peeps out enigmatically from, gestures, words, signs and prophecies, until in each specific case the end makes the connection with the beginning plan…. The co-incidence between the seen and the unseen becomes accomplished fact in the cycle…. No Greek historian would close his work with a glance into the future, as we are so prone to do …. As we understand the terms, the world of history and historic time are unknown to antiquity.[9]

Having in mind this understanding of time, which Israel had, we can turn to their understanding of history.

For ancient cultures the history was based primary upon their cult. This was also true for Israel. The history was arranged around the yearly festivals that she celebrated. They were the reminders of the saving acts of God which he did on behalf of his people. Hence, history for Israel was directly connected with God and his work with Israel. However next to this cultic understanding of history Israel inaugurated a linear understanding of history also based on God's deeds for Israel. The difference between the two concepts was that in the latter the reminder of God's deeds for Israel has been made relevant for every new generation and new historical time. That understanding of history did not have any analogy in the nations surrounding Israel.

Upon this understanding of history prophets developed the eschatological part of their messages. The eschatological nature of their messages was shaped by "an expectation of something soon to happen."[10] This is different from the 20th Century definition of eschatology, which content is "the consummation of the historical process in events which lie beyond the scope of the world's history."[11] However, since the prophets did not have our liner understanding of time they viewed the coming events as

---

[9] Karl Reinhardt, Herodotus Persergeschichte, in geistige Uberdieferung, hsg. v. E. Grassi, Berlin 1940, pp. 141ff, quoted in von Rad, 102.

[10] Ibid., 115.

[11] Ibid., 114.

final even when according to us they lay within the history. For the prophets the coming things were the things which God would do in connection with Israel. Thus, the crucial eschatological theme of their messages became "the new thing". It is best presented by the concept of the two aeons, which leads firmly to a dualistic understanding of history, which is definitely present in prophetic writings. The core of the concept of the two aeons is "the break which is preceded by Yahweh's great act of demolition and followed by the new state of things which he brings about."[12] In other words, the present condition of things will be changed by Yahweh's great act of extermination, and a new state of things will come to existence. According to von Rad it is not so important that we view God's new act in history as different from his old acts and title it eschatological, namely lying on the end of history or beyond it. What is important is "the break which goes so deep that the new state beyond it cannot be understood as the continuation of what went before."[13] Thus the prophets in order to introduce those new things, which God would do, first created a vacuum preaching for judgment, which removed the false security of Israel, and then presented the coming new things of God. However, the prophetic message preserved both the discontinuity and the continuity with the Israel's former election traditions.

> On the one hand, we see with what force and ardor the prophets catch up these election traditions in their preaching; on the other hand, their relationship to them is a broken one; for they regard the coming judgment as sealing the end of Israel's present existence; the security given her by these election traditions is cancelled out because of her guilt. The only thing she can hold on to is a new historical act on the part of Yahweh, the outlines of which the prophets already see, and to which they point with kindled emotions.

---

[12] Mowinckel, *He That Cometh,* p.125. J. Lindblom, "Gibt es eine Eschagologie bei den alttestamentlichen Propheten?" in *Studia Theologica,* 6 (1952), p. 79, quoted in Gerhard von Rad, 115.

[13] Ibid., 115.

> The prophetic message differs from all previous Israelite theology, which was based on the past saving history, in that the prophets looked for the decisive factor in Israel's whole existence-her life or her death-in some future event. Even so, the specific form of the new thing which they herald is not chosen at random; the new is to be affected in a way which is more or less analogous to God's former saving work.[14]

Thus, even though for the prophets there was discontinuity between the present and the future age, the continuity between the two still existed; they kept the analogy between God's new act of salvation for Israel and his formal saving deeds.

Next to von Rad's understanding of prophetic eschatology and its general framework of the two aeons, we should consider some other views relating to the latter. John F. A. Sawyer understands prophetic eschatology as related to the prophetic concept of "the day of the Lord."[15] This concept speaks clearly about the expectations and the predictions of the prophets about the future of Israel and of the whole world. As Sawyer sees it, the concept is built by two facets: first, it is "a prediction about God's ultimate victory over injustice and oppression;"[16] and second, it is a prediction about "the inauguration of the wonderful new age, in which there will be no more wars (Is 2:4; cf. 11:6-9), and prosperity and security for ever (e.g. Amos 9:13-15)."[17] Thus, the eschatological perspective of the prophets is clear. "The present age will come to an end; there is a complete break in history; and a new heaven and a new earth are brought into being (e.g. Is 65:6; Rev

---

[14] Ibid., 117.

[15] Geerhardus Vos argues that the phrase "the day of the Lord" is not only significant of understanding prophetic eschatology but it serves as proof for pre-prophetic eschatology." Geerhardus Vos, *Biblical Theology: Old and New Testament* (Grand Rapids, Michigan: WM. B. Eerdmans Publishing company, 1948), 313.

[16] John F. A. Sawyer, *Prophecy and the Prophets of the Old Testament*, Publication of Oxford Bible Series, eds. P. R. Ackroyd and G. N. Stanton (Oxford: Oxford University Press, 1987), 59.

[17] Ibid., 60.

21:2)."[18] Hence, the eschatological viewpoint of the prophets suggests plain understanding of the time and history as constructed by two ages/two worlds. The new age/new world is approaching imminently. It will replace the existing evil age/world. Furthermore, according to Sawyer, the roots of the concept of "the day of the Lord" can be found in two of Israel's contexts, namely historical and liturgical. The historical context refers to the stories which Israel told about Yahweh who has fought for Israel in her battles (e.g. Exod 14-15; Josh 10:8-14; Judg 5:20). The liturgical refers to "the myth about a struggle between God and some cosmic monster (e.g. Is 27:1; 51:9-10; Ps 89:9-10; 93; 74:13f.)."[19] The myth is called by D. S. Russell "the monster myth." He argues that it stays behind the creation story or the acts of God in creation and also behind the acts of God in history or God's delivery deeds in behalf of Israel. Furthermore, it is viewed by Russell, as staying even behind the acts of God at the end time.[20] This myth is found in Canaan and Babylonian primitive traditions. It exposes the combat between god (god of creation) and the great sea monster (known by different names).[21] Thus, those roots are connected directly to the concept of "the day of the Lord" and indirectly to the concept of the two aeons. Lying on this background, the eschatological perspective of the prophets could be seen as established on the concept of the two aeons. Another scholar who views the eschatology of the prophets established on this concept is Walter Brueggemann.

Brueggemann expresses the appearance of two-age concept in the framework of prophetic mediation of Yahweh. Two themes, according to him, are the best tools for summarization of this subject and in general of

---

[18] Ibid.

[19] Ibid., 59.

[20] "On that day the Lord with his cruel sword,

   his mighty and powerful sword, will punish

   Leviathan that twisting sea serpent,

   That writhing serpent Leviathan;

He will slay the monster of the deep" (Is 27:1 REB), quoted in D. S. Russell, *Prophecy and the Apocalyptic Dream: Protest and Promise* (Peabody, MA: Hendrickson Publishers, Inc, 1994), 49.

[21] D. S. Russell, *Prophecy and the Apocalyptic Dream: Protest and Promise*, 47-49.

summarization of its framework. Those two themes are ethics and eschatology.[22] The prophets spoke about the ethical present reality of Israel and about the future Yahweh's acts of newness. Their ethical messages of the present behavior of Israel were based on the Mosaic tradition. Their eschatological messages, on the other hand, laid on "Yahweh's circumstance-defying capacity to work newness."[23] Thus, the prophets make different emphasis on their eschatological messages, such as: Isaiah presents "a royally shaped future" (Is 9:2-7; 11:1-9); Jeremiah presents "Torah-centered future" (Jer 31:31-34); Ezekeil stresses a future of "stark holiness that attends to Yahweh's honor" (Ezek 36:22-32; 39:25-29). Although the prophets have their own unique outlook of the future their main point is to present Yahweh as the one whom independently from Israel's present circumstances will inaugurate a wonderful future for his people Israel and also for the world as a whole.[24]

In summary our attempt to analyze prophetic eschatology within the body of prophetic tradition with the goal of tracing the origins and development of the concept of the two aeons led to the following results. First, shaped by Israel's understanding of history and time and with a firmly established important place within the prophetic tradition, prophetic eschatology introduced the concept of the two aeons to the prophetic audience. Second, the core of the concept is the total break between the former state of the condition of Israel and the new state introduced by the great act of Yahweh, in other words, the break up between this aeon and the future aeon. Third, the continuity and discontinuity between the former history of Israel and the future new state of the history of the nation and the world in general are interwoven in the prophetic massages. Thus, the new age is decisively different from the old age and at the same time the former carries some of the features of the latter. God is still dealing primarily with Israel and he acts on her behalf in the mode closely linked with his former saving acts, but Israel is not anymore under the protection of the former election tradition and passing through God's judgment she will enter a new state of her history. The concept of the two aeons is clearly presented and

---

[22] Also James Robert Ross, 232.

[23] Walter Brueggemann, *Theology of the Old Testament: Testimony, Dispute, Advocacy* (Minneapolis: Fortress Press, 1997), 646.

[24] Ibid., 643-649.

developed by the prophets, but it neither originates from them nor is it completely matured in their writings. Its roots are traced further in the Canaan and Babylonian primitive traditions.

B. APOCALYPTIC ESCHATOLOGY

Apocalyptic literature, according to George J. Reid, "furnishes the completing links in the progress of Jewish theology and fills what would otherwise be a gap, though a small one, between the advanced stage marked by the deuterocanonical books and its full maturity in the time of Our Lord...."[25] It replaced the prophetic tradition, which was already dead, and firmly established its beginnings upon it and upon the Pentateuch. "It clothed itself fictitiously with the authority of a patriarch or prophet who was made to reveal the transcendent future."[26] Apocalyptic writings originated in the time of distress and despair for the Jewish people. They brought "both a message of comfort and an effort to solve the problems of the sufferings of the just and the apparent hopelessness of a fulfillment of the prophecies of Israel's sovereignty on earth."[27] The general question which was postulated and attempted to be answered through the Apocalyptic writings was "how to overcome the discrepancy between what is and what should be?"[28] Further and much more specific identification of the origins of the Apocalyptic writings is served by Ploeger and Hanson. They argue that the Apocalypticism has originated in the time of crisis in Jewish community, crisis that was reflected in the two main groups of people. They are called by Ploeger "theocratic party" and "eschatological party," and by Hanson hierocratic and visionary parties. Basically because of the tension between those two parties and as a fruit of the writings of the latter one, the Apocalyptic literature originated.[29]

---

[25] George J. Reid, *Apocrypha*, trans. by Douglas J. Potter, Dedicated to the Sacred Heart of Jesus Christ [database on-line] (From the Catholic Encyclopedia, copyright © 1913 by the Encyclopedia Press, Inc. Electronic version copyright © 1997 by New Advent, Inc, accessed 1 March).

[26] Ibid.

[27] Ibid.

[28] J. Christiaan Beker, *Paul's Apcalyptic Gospel: The Coming Triumph of God* (Philadelphia: Fortress Press, 1982), 30.

[29] Gerald F. Hawthorne and Ralph P. Martin, eds. *Dictionary of Paul and His Letters* (Leicester, England: Inter - Varsity Press, 1993), s.v. "Apocalypticism," by D. E. Aune.

Part I. Origins and Development of the Two Aeons Concept in Prophetic and Apocalyptic Traditions

Our first task in this section of our research is to define the term "Apocalyptic." Thus, we will serve our purposes through the definition offered by von Rad. The German scholar presents a widely accepted definition of the term "Apocalyptic." "It is a literary phenomenon of late Judaism, that is to say, the group of pseudepigraphical apocalypses from Daniel to IV Ezra."[30] However he finds this definition as inadequate. And although he agrees that Apocalyptic is a literary phenomenon in Judaistic literature, he points to the missing part of the definition, namely the theological phenomenon. Thus, he defines the Apocalyptic not purely as a literary phenomenon but also as a theological phenomenon which exposes the unique worldview of the Apocalyptic writers and the *Sitz im Leben* of their writings in Israel's context.[31]

D. E. Aune speaks about "Apocalypticism," as a general title embracing everything connected with the Apocalyptic tradition, namely its eschatology, behavior, literature, and motives. According to him it is "a worldview which characterized segments of early Judaism from c.200 B.C. to A.D. 200."[32] Its main content consists of visions, dreams and cosmic secrets through which Apocalyptists presented God's eschatological plans related to his people and the world. Speaking in general terms the main message of the Apocalyptists was that God would enter abruptly into human history in order to save his people and punish their enemies. Aune lists the following works as constructing the corpus of the Apocalypticism: Daniel 7-12 (the only OT Apocalypse), the five documents which comprise 1 Enoch (1-36, the Book of Watchers; 37-71, the Similitudes of Enoch; 72-82, the Book of Heavenly Luminaries; 83-90, the Animal Apocalypse; 92-104, the Epistle of Enoch), 2 Enoch, 4 Ezra, 2 Baruch, 3 Baruch, the Apocalypse of Abraham; the two early Christian Apocalypses; the Revelation of John (the only NT Apocalypse) and the Shepherd of Hermas. According to Aune, as we saw before, four segments construct the Apocalypticism, one of which is Apocalyptic eschatology. We may question, however, whether we can speak about Apocalyptic eschatology

---

[30]Ibid., 301. Also J. Christiaan Beker, 30.

[31] Gerhard von Rad, 302.

[32] Gerald F. Hawthorne and Ralph P. Martin, eds. *Dictionary of Paul and His Letters*, s.v. "Apocalypticism," by D. E. Aune.

only as a part of the Apocalypticism since the nature of the Apocalyptic messages and their content in general, as suggested before by Aune himself, are eschatological. Moreover, even he himself narrows the concept and speaks only about Apocalyptic eschatology using the term Apocalypticism to refer only to it. Thus, acknowledging that Apocalyptic literature has portions which are not primarily eschatological we should also affirm that Apocalypticism by its nature is eschatological. Hence, we should not divorce eschatology from Apocalypticism and discuss them separately. Therefore, the following definitions of Apocalyptic eschatology should be added to the definition given before about the Apocalyptic literature as a whole. Aune defines Apocalyptic eschatology as "characterized by the tendency to view reality from the perspective of divine sovereignty."[33] Hanson gives us a longer definition.

> Apocalyptic eschatology we define as a religious perspective which focuses on the disclosure (usually esoteric in nature) to the elect of the cosmic vision of Yahweh's sovereignty-especially as it relates to his acting to deliver his faithful-which disclosure the visionaries have largely ceased to translate into the terms of plain history, real politics, and human instrumentality due to a pessimistic view of reality growing out of the bleak post-exilic conditions within which those associated with the visionaries found themselves. Those conditions seemed unsuitable of them as a context for the envisioned restoration of Yahweh's people.[34]

Our second task is to expose the main traits of the Apocalyptic literature. We have several main characteristics, which are accepted by many of the scholars who are doing research in this area:

---

[33] Ibid.
[34] Paul D. Hanson, 11.

1. The doctrine of the two ages with its radical dualism
2. Pessimism and otherworldly hope, governed by the sense of the radical discontinuity between this age and the coming age
3. The division of time into segments or periods (four, seven, or twelve periods) according to a prefixed and determined plan of history
4. The imminent expectation of the kingdom of God, involving the overthrow of all earthly conditions and taking place by an act issuing from the throne of God
5. A cosmic, universal scope, where the individual no longer appears as a member of a collective entity and the end appears as a vast cosmic catastrophe
6. A new salvation for the faithful remnant, paradisiacal in character, arising beyond the catastrophe
7. The introduction of angels and demons to explain historical events and the happenings of the end time
8. The introduction of a mediator with royal functions[35]

---

[35] The following authors agree that these are the basic traits of the Apocalyptic literature:
P. Vielhauer, "Introduction," in *New Testament Apocrypha*, 581-607; Klaus Koch, *The Rediscovery of Apocalyptic* (SBT 2/22; Naperville, IL: Allenson, 1972) 18-35; L. Morris, *Apocalyptic* (Grand Rapids, MI: Eerdmans, 1972) 32-70; W. Schmithals, *The Apocalyptic Movement. Introduction and Interpretation* (New York: Abingdom, 1975) 29-49; and J. Collins, "Introduction. Towards the Morphology of a Genre," *Semeia 14. Apocalypse: The Morphology of a Genre* (ed. J. Collins; Chico, CA: Scholars, 1979) 1-20, quoted in Vincent P Branick, "Apocalyptic Paul?" *Catholic Biblical Quarterly 47* (October, 1985): 665.

Some further characteristics, which mark the uniqueness of the Apocalyptic theology, are exposed by von Rad. Predeterminism is the Apocalyptic idea that all the final events are determined in the past by God and are disclosed to a particular people a long time before they are going to happen. Hence, Apocalyptists wrote down those details far before their fulfillment in the future. However, they did not reveal their writings to others but concealed them. Those determined last events may be known only to those who are "initiated in understanding the art of decoding these predictions." Thus, we are introduced to the so-called esotericism and gnosticism. Moreover, the idea of "mystery and secret" is always present in Apocalyptic writings.[36]

According to Aune those main features of the Apocalypticism underline its main scenarios. Thus, our final goal in this section would be to analyze the nature and the place of the doctrine of the two aeons in the main body of characteristics of the Apocalypticism and also show how the former concept builds the Apocalyptic scenarios. Aune argues that the doctrine of the two ages, this age and the age to come, is the framework of Apocalyptic scenarios.[37] Von Rad as well determines it as the first and the foundational feature[38] of the Apocalyptic theology. Moreover, the doctrine of the two aeons shapes the whole understanding of the Apocalyptic writers about history. Thus, the doctrine does not only establish the framework of the Apocalyptic writings but furnishes their historical outlook. Apocalyptists viewed history as a divisible whole, containing two main stages, namely this aeon and the future aeon. This aeon, on another hand, is divided into several "times and seasons."[39] The future aeon is completely

---

[36] Gerhard von Rad, 302.

[37] Gerald F. Hawthorne and Ralph P. Martin, eds. *Dictionary of Paul and His Letters*, s.v. "Apocalypticism," by D. E. Aune. See also D. S. Russell, *Prophecy and the Apocalyptic Dream: Protest and Promise*, 28, 29.

[38] He places it in the framework of the eschatological dualism, and calls it "the clear-cut differentiation of the two aeons, the present one and one to come." Gerhard von Rad, 302.

[39] Sevenfold (I En 52; II En 33; T.L. 17). Twelvefold (II Bar 27; 56; 57; IV Ezra 11; 12; 14. William R. Murdock, 169. Also D. S. Russell, *From Early Judaism to Early Church*, 118, and John J. Collins, *Daniel with an Introduction to Apocalyptic Literature*, The Forms of the Old Testament Literature, eds. Rolf

detached from the present aeon and it enters the present aeon after the eschaton appears at the end of history.[40] However "…the present aeon is a space-time continuum that would eventually end and be succeeded by an eternal aeon."[41] The two aeons have three-dimensional nature. First, is a temporal, namely it defines the time as present and future. This age is the present time and the age to come is the future time which is going to come. Second, is spatial dimension or as von Rad calls it, transcendentalism. It postulates the two aeons in the spatial terms. This aeon, the present one, is the world down on the earth, the physical world. The coming aeon is the above-world in which "the saving blessings of the coming aeon are already pre-existent…" (Dan 7:13; Enoch 39: 3ff, 58:3,5, 59:2; 4 Ezra 13:36, etc)[42]

> The eschaton belonged essentially to this present aeon as its end. The future aeon, on the other hand, had existed contemporaneously with (although hidden to) this present aeon from the beginning;[43] and although the future aeon was not to be manifested to the righteous until this present aeon had been dissolved (i.e. until the eschaton) there was no essential connection between the two aeons not between the future aeon and the eschaton.[44]

Knierim and Gene M. Tucker, vol.20 (Grand Rapids, Michigan: William B. Eerdmans Publishing Company, 1984), 11, 12.

[40] "For behold, the days are coming when everything that has come into being will be given over to destruction, and it will be as if it had never been." (syr. Bar.31:5)

[41] William R. Murdock, "History and Revelation in Jewish Apocalypticism," *Interpretation: A Journal of Bible and Theology* (April 1967): 176.

[42] Gerhard von Rad, 302.

[43] Cf. IV Ezra 3:6; 7:26, 31; 9:18; 7:49; 8:1, 3; II Bar 51:8f.

[44] "This was made clear in those passages which suggest a time of cosmic purification between the two aeons (II En 33; II Bar 3:7; 44:9; IV Ezra 7:30- but denied in II Bar 4:1; IV Ezra 6:8-10)." William R. Murdock, 175. Furthermore, as William R. Murdock, argues the contrast between the two aeons is the best seen in, II Bar 44:8-f16; 48-50; 75; the Testaments of the Twelve Patriarchs (T. Judah

Third, the two aeons have qualitative dimension. The present aeon is "temporary and perishable," and the future aeon is "imperishable and eternal."[45] That dimension of the two aeons concept appears as early as Daniel. There the author presents the contrast between the earthly kingdoms and the heavenly kingdom. The latter, expressed by the picture of the falling from heaven stone or by the Son of man, crushed the former and established the eternal kingdom (Dan 2 and 7).

> You continued looking until a stone was cut out without hands, and it struck the statue on its feet of iron and clay and crushed them." "In the days of those kings the God of heaven will set up a kingdom which will never be destroyed, and *that* kingdom will not be left for another people; it will crush and put an end to all these kingdoms, but it will itself endure forever...." "Then I kept looking because of the sound of the boastful words which the horn was speaking; I kept looking until the beast was slain, and its body was destroyed and given to the burning fire. As for the rest of the beasts, their dominion was taken away, but an extension of life was granted to them for an appointed period of time. I kept looking in the night visions, And behold, with the clouds of heaven One like a Son of Man was coming, And He came up to the Ancient of Days and was presented before Him. And to Him was given dominion, Glory and a kingdom, that all the peoples, nations and *men of every* language might serve Him. His dominion is an everlasting dominion which will not pass away; And His kingdom is one Which will not be destroyed. "But the saints of the Highest One will

---

25f.; T.L. 18); I En (16; 25; 38; 39; 45; 41; 53; 56; 58; 62; 71; 72; 91); II En 33; 50:2; 65-66). William R. Murdock, 176.

[45] P. Vielhauer, "Introduction," in *New Testament Apocrypha*, 588.

> receive the kingdom and possess the kingdom forever, for all ages to come. (Dan 2:34, 44; 7:11-14, 18)

In the later Apocalyptic literature (4 Esra and syr. Bar.) that dimension of the two aeons is plainly exposed.[46]

Hence, established in the framework of the doctrine of the two aeons and furnished with the two aeons historical outlook we have the following Apocalyptic scenarios. This age is an evil age during which the devil and his human accomplices are ruling over the world. During this age the people of God are few and in sufferings they anticipate the coming of the new age. The new age arrives with the decisive act of God. The final battle is conducted right before the end of the evil age. God together with his servants demolish the armies of Satan.[47] "This conquest could be described as an eschatological war in which Satan and his host of demonic and human followers would be finally defeated by the host of angels and righteous men under the command of God. '…the Lord God shall appear on earth, and Himself save men. Then shall all the spirits of deceit be given to be trodden under foot'… (T.S. 6:5-6)"[48] Immediately after that, the new age is inaugurated, the condition of all things is changed and the world comes back to its perfect order which corresponds to what was in Eden. Of course, all of these details have been predetermined by God and there was not any doubt that the powers of evil would be destroyed; the old age with its formal stage of sin is erased, and the new age with its condition of bliss and complete perfection of all things is established forever under the reign of God and his chosen agent Messiah.[49]

We should consider as well, from the standpoint of Apocalyptists, where the roots of the two aeons doctrine lie. As Murdock holds on, those

---

[46] P. Vielhauer, "Introduction," in *New Testament Apocrypha*, 588.

[47] Gerald F. Hawthorne and Ralph P. Martin, eds. *Dictionary of Paul and His Letters*, s.v. "Apocalypticism," by D. E. Aune. See also D. S. Russell, *Prophecy and the Apocalyptic Dream: Protest and Promise*, 28, 29.

[48] William R. Murdock, 178.

[49] Gerald F. Hawthorne and Ralph P. Martin, eds. *Dictionary of Paul and His Letters*, s.v. "Apocalypticism," by D. E. Aune. See also D. S. Russell, *Prophecy and the Apocalyptic Dream: Protest and Promise*, 28, 29.

roots are firmly situated in the Iranian-Babylonian syncretism. The latter has developed the understanding of history based on the two aeons concept. It viewed history as a divisible whole. It "divides this present aeon into periods of one thousand years, either seven or twelve, corresponding to the planets or the signs of the zodiac respectively."[50] The main goal of such understanding is to present "that the duration of this aeon is fixed and temporally resolved by the heavens."[51] Furthermore as in Apocalypticism "for Iranian parallelism this present aeon was created by God, and it was the sphere of conflict between the divine and the demonic. As this present aeon grew older, it would fall progressively under the dominion of Beliar, "who is the ruler of this world."[52] At the end of history lies the eschaton which marks the end of this present evil aeon and establishes the beginning of the new aeon.[53] The new aeon introduces the eternal order of things in which the evil is erased completely.

In summary, Apocalypticism should be understood as literary and theological phenomenon of Judaistic literature which originated in the time of crisis of Israel's community and focused on the relationship between the present and future time. The nature of that phenomenon is primarily eschatological and its core doctrine and general framework is the concept of the two aeons. Furthermore, the concept of the two aeons is three-dimensional and presents the view of history divided on two parts without any connection between each other. The three dimensions of the concept are spatial, temporal, and qualitative. In other words, they present the two aeons as this world and the world above, this age and the age to come, and the present temporary and perishable world and the future imperishable and eternal world. Thus, we may conclude that the concept of the two aeons has its crucial place in the Apocalypticism but does not originate from it. Its roots are traced further in Iranian-Babylonian syncretism.

With this understanding of the concept of the two aeons as formulated, understood, and used by Apocalyptists, we are ready to move further toward the discussion of the relationship between the prophetic and Apocalyptic eschatology in relation to the doctrine under consideration.

---

[50] William R. Murdock, 169.

[51] Ibid., 169.

[52] Ibid., 177.

[53] Ibid., 177-179.

Part I. Origins and Development of the Two Aeons Concept in Prophetic and Apocalyptic Traditions

C. CONTINUITY AND DISCONTINUITY BETWEEN PROPHETIC AND APOCALYPTIC ESCHATOLOGIES IN RELATION TO THE TWO AEONS CONCEPT

Our introductory task of this section will be to establish the relationship between Prophecy and Apocalypticism in general. Von Rad states that some of the features of Apocalyptic literature are found in prophetic tradition, such as "keen interest to the last things and the significance that it attaches to visions and dreams." Hence some have determined Apocalyptic as "a child of the prophecy."[54] However von Rad disagrees with this definition of the relation between Apocalypticism and prophecy. For him there is more discontinuity between the two traditions than continuity.

First, von Rad argues that the Apocalyptic literature never defines itself as prophecy, but to the contrary it speaks about the prophecy as ended ("the prophets have fallen asleep," Syr. Baruch 75:3). Second, for him the most crucial distinction between the two genres is the understanding of history. The Apocalyptists viewed history apart from the formal salvation tradition of Israel. What they did is that they changed it completely by turning it to allegory in the form of code. They completely overlooked the history of Israel and presented the history of the world as a whole under the future divine actions. On the other hand, the prophets built their messages upon the old Israel's tradition of God's salvific deeds which he performed in her behalf in the past. "For Israel, history was the place in which she experienced her election by Yahweh and from which she alone could understand her own identity. No generation was exempted from that task; each one in succession was obliged to achieve this self-understanding in faith."[55] However von Rad has managed to ignore the influence of that view

---

[54] O. Procksch, *Theologie des Alten Testaments*, Gutersloh 1950, p.401; H. H. Rowley, *The Relevance of Apocalyptic*, 2nd edn. Henceforth cited as *Apocalyptic*, London and Redhill 1947, p.13, quoted in D. S. Russell, *From Early Judaism to Early Church* (Philadelphia: Fortress Press, 1986), 44. Also D. S. Russell, *From Early Judaism to Early Church* (Philadelphia: Fortress Press, 1986), 44.

[55] Gerhard von Rad, 303.

of history upon the Apocalyptists. As Murdock[56] recognizes it, the prophets influenced some of the early Apocalyptists by the idea of the earthly kingdom as the expression of the eschaton at the end of history. Thus, those Apocalyptists spoke about the earthly kingdom instead of eschaton, and even some of them presented the earthly kingdom followed by the new aeon.[57] Moreover D. S. Russell argues that the Apocalyptists "took very seriously indeed not only the historical events of their own day, but also all the generations that had gone before."[58] Furthermore von Rad forgets his formal claim about the discontinuity of prophetic eschatology with the formal-election tradition of Israel.

Third, von Rad argues that the methods applied by prophets and Apocalyptists are different. Although the prophets used allegorical language it was not predominant in their writings as the Apocalyptic writers. They presented the world history in purely allegorical form. Forth, the view of the Apocalyptists, about the end of the world, was different from the prophetic view. The former viewed the end of the world as coming because of the increasing evil, the latter put the emphasis on God's intervention. Fifth, in their writings the prophets disclosed their position in the history from which they were writing; contrary the Apocalyptists have hidden it. Thus, von Rad finds another source for the origin of the Apocalyptic literature, namely the wisdom literature.

The main line of agreement between the two genres is the concept of knowledge. Knowledge is very important both for wisdom literature and for Apocalyptic literature. In wisdom literature we identify the "effort made by the people of Israel to grasp the laws which governed the world in which she lived, and to systematize them."[59] Thus, the developed system became later the main tool for understanding not only the natural

---

[56] William R. Murdock, 174, 175.

[57] I En 10:17-22; 24:1-25:7; 28:1-32:6; 45: 51:4-5; 53:7 (?); 90:20-42 (?); T.L. 18:22; T.D. 5:10-3; T. Joseph 19. The following Apocalyptists viewed the earthly kingdom preceded the new aeon: II Bar 6:9; Bar 29:3-30:1; 72:2; IV Ezra 7:26-30.

[58] D. S. Russell, *From Early Judaism to Early Church* (Philadelphia: Fortress Press, 1986), 117.

[59] Gerhard von Rad, 306.

philosophy but also the history. This, according to von Rad, is another main feature of the Apocalyptic literature next to the concept of the two aeons.

> And are not the matters with which Apocalyptic literature is occupied expressly those of wisdom and its science? In the Apocalypse of Enoch there is an enormous accumulation of knowledge about the development of civilization (Enoch 8), the heavenly bodes (Enoch 72-79), the calendar, meteorology, and geography….Daniel is educated as a wise man (Dan 1:3ff) and in consequence he is enrolled among the wise men (Dan 2:48); charismatic wisdom gives him his ability to interpret dreams (Dan 2:30, 5:2), and his Book, which contains an 'almost overwhelming admixture of erudition,' actually ends with an apotheosis of the Wisdom teachers (Dan 12:3). Enoch designates himself as a unique representative of true wisdom (Enoch 37:2-4), and Ezra, who had Apocalyptic knowledge granted him, I was called 'scribe of the knowledge of the Most High' (4 Ezra 14:50).[60]

In agreement with Aune and the majority of the scholars we should be reluctant to assert such a strong connection between the wisdom literature and Apocalypticism although there is a connection.[61] Moreover we should be reluctant to assume such a distinctive discontinuity between prophecy and apocalypitcism, although there is a discontinuity. Hence, in order to determine the exact relationship between prophecy and apocalypitcism we should proceed in discussing the relation between prophetic and Apocalyptic eschatologies.

Our main task of this section is to look at the relationship between the Prophetic and Apocalyptic eschatologies. Paul D. Hanson attempts to

---

[60] Ibid.

[61] Gerald F. Hawthorne and Ralph P. Martin, eds. *Dictionary of Paul and His Letters*, s.v. "Apocalypticism," by D. E. Aune.

define the basic discontinuity and continuity between prophetic and Apocalyptic eschatologies. He argues that the discontinuity appeared in the relation between the messages of the writers of the two genres to the present political and historic reality. Prophets presented the salvation acts of Yahweh of restoring Israel in the framework of their present politico-historic reality. On the other hand, the Apocalyptists presented Yahweh's salvation actions in restoring his people detached from the politico-historical realm. However, the main continuity, which Hanson asserts, is found in the main subject of both eschatologies. This is "the restoration of Yahweh's people as a holy community in a glorified Zion."[62] Carl E. Armerding agrees with this claim from the standpoint of the prophets. He affirms that the prophetic message was engaged with the future of Israel.

> That the prophets looked for a day of Israel's restoration is plain, though numerous contemporary writers seem oblivious to the fact that many of the prophecies were fulfilled in the restoration under Zerubbabel, Ezra, and Nehemiah. But there is another dimension to Israel's restoration, and that is found in the exalted language that points to a day when universal peace and justice will mark the earth.[63]

However, the scholars disagree with that claim of Hanson from the standpoint of Apocalyptic eschatology. Thus, Murdock argues that "in the case of Apocalypticism, however, one no longer has to do with the historical destiny of a nation, but with the eternal destiny of individuals."[64]

---

[62] Paul D. Hanson, 12.

[63] Carl E. Armerding, "Prophecy in the Old Testament," in *Handbook of Biblical Prophecy*, eds. Carl E. Armerding and W. Ward Gasque (Grand Rapids, Michigan: Baker Book House, 1977), 68.

[64] He gives the following quotations for proof: "IV Ezra 7:5-69; 'Perish, then, the multitude which has been born in vain; but let my grape be preserved, and my plant, which with much labor I have perfected!' IV Ezra 9:22; IV Ezra 5:40. Murdock also substantiates his claim with the work of R. Bultmann, "Geschichte und Eschatologie im Neuen Testament," *Glauben und Verstehen*,

And P. Vielhauer claims that in their eschatological outlook of the future age Apocalyptists are not concerned with the Palestine and Jerusalem but with the whole of the cosmos, namely earth, heaven, and the underworld. "Within this cosmic-universal framework the Jewish people do not play the central and sustaining role it does in the national eschatology..."[65] Furthermore, Hanson himself speaks about the plain universalism which appeared in the writings of Third Isaiah (Is 60:21a; 61:6a) and Zechariah 9-14 (Zech 9:20, 21).[66] Thus, his earlier claim should be viewed in the light of his latter claim. It is clear that Hanson contradicts himself. In order to resolve this obvious discrepancy, we need to reject his earlier claim and to make a new assertion. Hanson understands the writings of the Third Isaiah and Zechariah 9-14 as the bridge between the classical prophecy and Apocalypticism, an issue that we will substantiate latter. They are moving astray from the prophetic eschatology which views the future as primary preoccupied with the nation of Israel. Thus, they introduce the universalistic line of thinking which is developed latter on in the Apocalyptic eschatology. To assure ourselves with the appropriateness of our assertion we will provide an argument from Hanson himself. He states that "it is no accident that the collapse of the political aspects of the prophetic office is followed closely by strong expressions of universalism unprecedented in earlier biblical tradition (Is 56:3-8; 66:18-23; Zech 14:16, 20-21; Mal 1:11)."[67]

Furthermore, contrary to von Rad, Hanson views the roots of Apocalypticism in prophetic tradition. He argues for two main periods of formation of the Apocalyptic tradition from the prophetic tradition, namely six-fifth century BC and second century BC. In particular he defines four main traits which underline the development of the Apocalyptic eschatology from the classic prophecy.

> (1) the sources of Apocalyptic eschatology lie solidly
> within the prophetic tradition of Israel; (2) the period

Vol. III (Tubingen: J. C. B. Mohr [Paul Siebeck], 1962), pp.91-106, esp.p.94; The Presence of Eternity (New York: Harper and Brothers, 1957), p.31.

[65] P. Vielhauer, "Introduction," in *New Testament Apocrypha*, 590.

[66] Paul D. Hanson, 387.

[67] Ibid., 396.

> of origin is in the sixth to the fifth centuries; (3) the essential nature of Apocalyptic is found in the abandonment of the prophetic task of translating the vision of the divine council into historical terms; (4) the historical and sociological matrix of Apocalyptic is found in an inner-community struggle in the period of the Second Temple between visionary and hierocratic elements.[68]

Due to the fact that Hanson sees the bridge between Apocalyptic literature and prophetic tradition in the community struggle between visionary and hierocratic drifts in Israel we need to look at how he defines these groups and their relationship. Those groups were formed in the period after the exile, called post-exilic period. Their features could be defined on a basis of the accounts found in Isaiah 60-62 and Ezekiel 40-48. Hanson believes that these two passages are the programs for the restoration of Israel which these two groups developed and supported. The group of visionaries, Isaiah 60-62, "fervently longed for divine intervention to usher in a radically new order, and on the basis of their vision of an ideal new age to come, they proclaimed judgement upon existing structures."[69] According to Hanson this group has been "referred to as the prophetic tradition, inasmuch as its inspirations derived from the prophets, and even down to late Apocalyptic its kinship to prophecy is evident."[70] The group of hierocratic or realists, Ezekiel 40-48, were the leaders of the existing religious and institutional structures, which they defended and preserved with painstaking effort, maintaining "the day-to-day life of the temple community."[71] Those two groups were in general conflict even though they mutually built the common faith of Israel.

> These contrasting mentalities are brought into sharp
> focus when one compares the corresponding details

---

[68] Ibid., 29.

[69] Ibid., 71, footnote 44.

[70] Ibid., 72.

[71] Ibid.

within the two programs: (1) The leaders of the prophetic community are Peace and Righteousness (Is 60:17b), those of the hierocracy are the various officials of the priestly and civil hierarchies, headed by he high priest and the prince. (2) The promise of the visionary is that the whole nation 'will be named the priests of Yahweh, the ministers of our God' (61:6); the realist carefully regulates; '… mark well those who may be admitted to the temple and all those who are to be excluded from the sanctuary…; [the Levites] shall not come near to me, to serve me as priests…" (44:5, 13); '… the sons of Zadok… alone among the sons of Levi may come near to the Lord to minister to him' (40:46; cf. 44:14). (3) The visionary exults, 'Your people shall all be righteous…' (60:12); the realists meticulously explains that holiness is reserved for the few and that it must be safeguarded by ordinances: when the Zadokites leave the inner court, 'they shall put off the garments in which they have been ministering, and lay them in the holy chambers; and they shall put on other garments, lest they communicate holiness to the people with their garments…. They shall teach my people the difference between the holy and the common…' (44:19, 23). A special holy place is designated where the priests are to boil the offerings, 'in order not to bring them out into the outer court and so communicate holiness to the people' (46:20). (4) The visionary announces: 'The glory of Lebanon will come to you, the cypress, the plane, and the pine together, to adorn the site of my sanctuary, that I may glorify the resting place of my feet' (60:13); the realist draws up architectural plans, exact in every detail, for the new temple, and lays it before the people to build it (43:10-12). (5) The visionary proclaims, 'Foreigners will rebuild you walls, and their kings will

> serve you,' whereas the attitude of the realist could be summarized in the old maxim: 'God helps those who help themselves.' [72]

One of the main outcomes of the tension of those two groups was their writings. For us the main interest deserves the writings of the visionaries since they established the main link between prophetic and Apocalyptic eschatology. Moreover, they were built upon the classical prophetic writings. They consist from the texts of Isaiah 56-66 and Zechariah 9-14.

Isaiah 44-55 or so called Duetero-Isaiah presents the promises of the restoration of Israel in the mode of keeping the balance between history and mythology.[73] However, this preserving of the balance was something which started to escape from the author of Deutero-Isaiah with the upholding of mythology versus history. The myth, which started to gain place in the writings of Deutero-Isaiah, was the cosmic myth of Divine-Warrior. This myth derived from mythical cycles of the Cannanites.[74]

Two examples of the structure of the myth can be served from "the cultic rituals celebrating the victory of the god of the thunderstorm in Canaan and Mesopotamia. The Cannanite version is from Ugaritic literature discovered at Ras Shamra. The Meopotamian version is *Enuma elis*, the classical formulation of West Semitic myth of Baal's battle with Yamm.

Cannanatie version:
Threat (2.1[137])
Combat-victory (2.4 [68])
Temple built (4 [51])
Banquet (4.6.39 ff [51])

---

[72] Ibid., 72-73.

[73] With the support of currently done research von Rad argues that the core of prophetic message is based upon the old tradition and shaped by the Ancient East concepts, which have been used in cults, myths, and magical ideas. (Gerhard von Rad, 4.)

[74] Paul D. Hanson, 302.

*Manifestation of Baal's Universal Reign
(anticipated: 2.4.9-10 [68]; manifested: 4.7.9.-12
[51])
Theophany of Divine Warrior (4.7.27-39 [51])
Fertility of Restored Order (anticipated: 4.5.68-71
[51]; effected: 4.7.18-30 [51]; cf. 6.3.6-7, 12-13
[49])*

Mesopotamian version:
Threat (I:109-II:91)
Combat-victory (IV: 33-122)
Theophany of Divine Warrior (IV: 39-60)
Salvation of the Gods (IV: 123-146; VI: 1-44; cf.
VI:126-127, 149-151)
Fertility of the Restored Order (V: 1-66; cf. VII: 1-2,
59-83)
Procession and Victory Shout (V: 67-89)
Temple Built for Marduk (V: 117-156; VI:45-68)
Banquet (VI: 69-94)
*Manifestation of Marduk's Universal Reign
(anticipated: IV:3-18; manifested: VI: 95-VII:144).*[75]

In both mythical structures, although the eschatological dualism is not clearly shown, it can be understood from the generalization of the structural whole presented by Hanson in the brackets. Thus, we have the first anticipation of the final bliss the manifestation, final victory and of the universal reign of a divine being and then we have the manifestation of these activities and their full consummation.

The cosmic myth of Divine-Warrior together with the royal ideology of Near Eastern kingship found their fulfillment in the royal cult of Jerusalem.[76] Thus, the myth contained the complete cosmological visionary of the Divine-Warrior and how he is fighting and overcoming evil. For Israel it was "the victory of Israel's Heavenly King in overcoming

---

[75] Paul D. Hanson, 302.
[76] Ibid., 126.

the dark powers of sterility, a victory which guaranteed the fertility of the land and the prosperity of the people."[77] The myth, namely "the saving cosmic activities of the Divine-Warrior and his council"[78] may be traced in Israel's religious history. "For instance, the early prophet Micaiah ben Imlah participated in this visionary element (1 Kings 22), relating it to the battle at Ramoth-gilead."[79] Furthermore the myth has been presented in the writings of the pre-exilic prophets even though hardly recognizable, since it has been well interwoven with the politico-historical core of their messages.[80] This myth was accommodated with Isaiah in First Isaiah who through it saw "the remarkable cosmic change throughout nature which Yahweh's new act would inaugurate."[81] That "led the prophet to divide history into two periods, the past, which was to be forgotten, and the future 'new thing' which Yahweh was about to perform (Is 43:18-19)."[82] That passage in First Isaiah became the background of the most crucial passage, which came up to be the core of the Apocalyptic literature, namely Isaiah 65:17-25. Hanson defines it as "a passage of paramount importance for the study of the development of prophetic eschatology into Apocalyptic eschatology." Exactly in that passage the doctrine of the two aeons is clearly stated.

> In this passage one of the cardinal doctrines of the Apocalyptic literature finds its earliest clear formulation, the doctrine of world epochs. In the delineation of the new heavens and new earth which would replace the old, the influence of mythical dualism, with its disparagement of the old world order in favor of the new order which would replace it, reaches a high water point within early Apocalyptic. It does not represent the end of the development of that doctrine, for later the two world epochs found here

---

[77] Ibid.

[78] Ibid., 16.

[79] Ibid.

[80] Ibid., 17, 18.

[81] Ibid., 127.

[82] Ibid.

splinter into a multiplicity of different stages. Nor does it mark the beginning of the development of that doctrine....[83]

Two further myths which have almost identical content with the Divine-Warrior myth and which are viewed by Russell as shaping the language of the Apocalyptic writings are the following: "the monster myth and the cosmos myth."[84] As we saw before, the first myth lies behind the creation account and also behind the other Old Testament writings including the prophetic once. One of the main figures of the myth is the monster that appears in two persons, namely Behemoth and Leviathan in some of the Apocalyptic writings and exactly in the passages with the eschatological context.

> On that day were two monsters parted, a female monster named Leviathan, to dwell in the abysses of the ocean over the fountains of the waters. But the male is named Behemoth, who occupied with his breast a waste wilderness.... And I besought the other angel that he should show me the might of those monsters, how they were parted on one day and cast, the one into the abysses of the sea, and the other into the dry land of the wilderness. (1 Enoch 60:7-9)[85]

> It will come to pass... that the Messiah will then begin to be revealed. And Behemoth will be revealed from his place, and Leviathan will ascend from the sea, those two great monsters which I created on the fifth day of creation, and I kept them until that time; and then they will be for food for all that are left. (2 Baruch 29:3-4)[86]

---

[83] Ibid., 155.

[84] D. S. Russell, *Prophecy and the Apocalyptic Dream: Protest and Promise*, 47-54.

[85] Quoted in D. S. Russell, *Prophecy and the Apocalyptic Dream: Protest and Promise*, 50, 51.

[86] Ibid.

Moreover another feature of the myth, the eschatological or messianic banquet, is "fairly widespread and is to be found in the Qumran texts and Rabbinic sources as well as in the New Testament (cf. Luke 13:28-29; 22:30ff.; Rev 19:9)."[87] The eschatological moment as seen in the whole picture of the myth as reflected in some of the Apocalyptic writings is that the evil powers consisting of Satan and his fallen angels who are dwelling in this world will be overcome by the righteous and their angelic protectors in the new age to come.[88] The other myth, the cosmos myth, comes from Mesopotamian context. It presents "the struggle here on earth between good and evil, which is to be understood in terms of a cosmic struggle in the heavenly realms between the powers of light and the powers of darkness."[89] This myth clearly "demonstrates a dualism that is both spatial (this present world over against the heavenly) and temporal (this historical scene over against the transcendent)."[90]

However, we should not think that we have fully developed the concept of the two aeons here in Isaiah, neither have we in Zechariah, as later Apocalyptic has it. Hanson even goes so far to say that in Zechariah 9 "all features of late Apocalyptic are lacking, such as the sharp dualism and the resulting division of history into aeons, and the cataclysmic disruption of the natural order heralding the eschaton in late Apocalyptic."[91] Thus, Aune also argues that the earliest occurrence of the phrase "the world to come" is located in 1 Enoch 71:15 (B.C. 200). Moreover, he claims that "the doctrine of the two ages is fully developed by 90 A.D., for according to 4 Ezra 7:50, 'the most High has not made one Age but two" (4 Ezra 8:1)."[92] According to him the concept of the two aeons developed only gradually in Judaism. However, Hanson does not hesitate to admit that even in Zechariah 9 "the description of the final bloody struggle against the foe couched in the language of myth and the

---

[87] D. S. Russell, *Prophecy and the Apocalyptic Dream: Protest and Promise*, 51.

[88] Ibid., 53.

[89] Ibid.

[90] Ibid.

[91] Paul D. Hanson, 323

[92] Gerald F. Hawthorne and Ralph P. Martin, eds. *Dictionary of Paul and His Letters*, s.v. "Apocalypticism," by D. E. Aune.

juxtaposition of passages like verses 4-9 and 10, and 14-15 and 16-17 adumbrate the dualism of later Apocalyptic."[93] Hence, it is thoroughly clear that in the literature of the visionaries we are witnesses of the early development of the concept of the two aeons in the Apocalyptico-prophetic literature. That understanding could be traced further by presenting the dualistico-Apocalyptic character of their writings through the synthesis which Hanson derives from Isaiah and Zechariah.

> The essential characteristics of Apocalyptic eschatology are drawn together into a coherent whole in Isaiah 65: the present era is evil; a great judgment separating the good from the evil and marking the crossroads between the present world and the world to come is imminent; a newly created world of peace and blessing ordained for the faithful lies beyond that judgment. These teachings of world epochs, universal judgment, and a modified dualism are the basic components of later Apocalyptic eschatology.[94]

> Restoration of Yahweh's true followers could no longer be envisioned within the present evil social and natural order. Therefore that day of restoration had to be preceded by a cosmic battle which would eliminate the enemies of wickedness who caused the fall of the world to evil, and then by a new creation intended to restore the world to a paradisiacal purity suitable as a context for the restoration. The dualism and the related doctrine of the two eras (seasons) of Near Eastern myth are here revitalized in the visionary tradition. This reconstruction does not strain phenomenological plausibility; when all of the assured structures of the past epoch have collapsed, to whom do the defeated and weary visionaries turn? To

---

[93] Paul D. Hanson, 323.
[94] Ibid., 160.

> Yahweh who will intervene to engage in battle with all of the hostile forces of the world, to Yahweh who will enter his holy city in a victorious procession accompanied by his holy ones, to Yahweh who will reorder the fallen creation into a new harmony free from the divided structures which no longer could support life, to Yahweh who 'will become king over all the earth, … who will be one and his name one.'[95]

The writings of the visionaries emphasized the mythical versus politico-historical-present reality. What is clear is that in all of them the main traits of the Apocalyptic eschatology are plainly visible and the concept of the two aeons is clearly stated. Those writings have been added to Deutero-Isaiah at the period following the missions of Nehemiah and Ezra, frequently called by the scholars Trito-Isaiah.[96] The other text, Zechariah 9-14 was attached to the collection of Minor Prophets at the same period as the text of Isaiah. Moreover, as we saw previously, and as Hanson affirms, the dualistic concept of the two aeons does originate neither from the prophets nor from Apocalyptists. Although it could be traced back to the Divine-Warrior myth of the Cannanite community and some other myths as the monster myth and the cosmos myth of Canaan, Babylonian, and Mesopotamian primitive traditions. Furthermore, it can be traced in the Iranian-Babylonian syncretism both in its understanding of history and its view of the eschaton as "making the shift from this present aeon to the future aeon."[97] Nevertheless, as we saw, the concept of the two aeons established a firm continuity between the prophetic and Apocalyptic eschatologies.

---

[95] Ibid., 379.
[96] Ibid., 127, 131, 400.
[97] William R. Murdock, 179.

D. CONCLUSION

On the basis of our previously presented discussion, we would like to conclude the first part of our research.

First, we found, throughout our research of the prophetic eschatology, that the concept of the two aeons is clearly present in it, but it does not originate from it. It is further traced in Canaan and Babylonian primitive traditions. Second, analyzing the Apocalyptic tradition we understood that the concept of the two aeons finds an important place in it and it is fully developed especially in the late Apocalypticism. Neither it does originate from it, but is further traced in Iranian-Babylonian syncretism. Finally, developing the relationship between the prophetic and Apocalyptic eshatologies we concluded that the concept of the two aeons established the firm continuity between the two eschatologies.

Nevertheless, we saw that von Rad overlooked the continuity between the prophetic and Apocalyptic traditions. However, his most crucial argument of discontinuity is weaken because of his inability to discern the continuity between the two traditions on the basis of their dualistic understanding of history in general and in their understanding of the concept of the two aeons in particular. Both groups of writers viewed the deep gap between the present age and the age to come settled by the Yahweh's great act of demolition. Even though there is a difference in the understanding of history and the relation to the Israel's election traditions it is not unparalleled. Von Rad argues, that the prophets did not abandon Israel's election traditions completely and that the Apocalyptists did, is even according to him not conclusive argument since he himself argues that the Apocalyptic authors also used Israel's traditions even though they altered them and used them in the form of allegorical language.

Even more contradictory than von Rad's argument is the claim of Russell. He argues that the concept of the two ages does not have any parallel in the prophetic writings. However, he himself affirms the roots of this concept in the ancient Near-East mythology and also sees this mythology not only as shaping the eschatological language of the prophets in some aspects but also shaping the language of some other passages from the Old Testament.

Moreover, both Hanson and Aune are not speaking about a full development of the concept of the two aeons before complete establishment of the Apocalyptic tradition. However, Aune recognizes that the concept has developed gradually in Judaism as a whole. And Hanson especially affirms the presence of the concept of the two aeons, although not in its final form, in the prophets. Moreover, he traces the roots of the concept through the ancient Near-East mythology and through it found it even in some Biblical-historical writings.

In conclusion, we can substantiate that the concept of the two aeons has originated or at least is traced as far as the ancient Near-East mythology. It is used by the prophets with the softened contrast between the two aeons. It is adapted, modified and used by the Apocalyptists as well; with the stronger contrast between the two aeons and with the strongly established three-dimensional nature, spatial, temporal, and qualitative. Thus, our attempt to unfold the origin and to trace the development of the two aeons concept in prophetic and Apocalyptic eschatologies has been successful. However, keeping the formal conclusion in our minds we need to proceed our examination of the two aeons concept further in First Century Judaism and Biblical literature.

PART II. DEVELOPMENT OF THE TWO AEONS CONCEPT IN FIRST CENTURY JUDAISM AND BIBLICAL LITERATURE

Our second main analysis will attempt to establish the development of the concept of the two aeons in the first century Judaism and Biblical literature. First, we will examine the understanding of the Rabbis related to the concept under consideration. Second, on the basis of the latter conclusions we will consider the New Testament understanding of the concept and analyze its development.

A. FIRST CENTURY RABBINICO-JEWISH ESCHATOLOGY

Turning to Judaism we find that its main eschatological framework was established on the Apocalyptic concept of the two aeons. W. D. Davies asserts that "the eschatology of the first century falls into the framework: this Present Age (ha-olam ha-zeh), the Messianic Era, and the Age to Come (ha-olam ha-ba)."[98] However, the scholars are divided about the presence of the Apocalyptic elements in the Rabbinic Judaism. On the one hand, Moore argues that apocalypticism has always laid outside of the main body of the Rabbinic literature. On the other hand, scholars as C. C. Torrey, Porter, and Charles, although in different language, affirm that Apocalypticism has its role in forming Rabbis theology and especially Rabbis eschatology.[99] John Strugnell goes even further claiming that the Apocalyptic writings of 2 Baruch, 4 Ezra and Pseudo-Philo (Biblical Antiquities) provide the direct evidence for Rabbinic Judaism. In the light of this argument Arthur J. Rerch would gather most of the scholars around the claim that "the thinking represented in 2 Baruch, 4 Ezra, and Biblical Antiquities is that of Pharisaic Judaism."[100] The basic eschatological timetable of those works is the already stated threefold scheme. This age

---

[98] W. D. Davies, *Paul and Rabbinic Judaism: Some Rabbinic Elements in Pauline Theology* (New York and Evanston: Harper and Row, Publishers, 1948), 288.

[99] W. D. Davies, 10.

[100] Arthur J. Ferch, 135.

started from the fall and reaches the eschaton. It is an evil age full of suffering and sorrow for the people of God. At the end of this aeon the Messianic age will take place. It is part of this aeon, that Messiah appears on the scene of history to deal with the Gentiles. After the Messianic age is completed (its length is different according to the particular author) Messiah either dies (4 Ezra) or is ascended to glory (2 Baruch). With the cessation of the Messianic age the new aeon is established. The inaugurating events are the judgement and the resurrection (4 Ezra 7:31-44). The new aeon is established, and even though its exact place is not clear (heaven or earth, depending on the particular writer), it is plainly stated by all of the authors that it is going to be everlasting.[101] For us, however, the most important thing is to see that the crucial element of the content of those Apocalyptic writings is the doctrine of the two aeons. Thus, the author of Pseudo-Philo states it clearly.

> But when the years of the world shall be fulfilled, then shall the light cease and the darkness vanish; and I will quicken the dead and raise up from the earth them that sleep; and Sheol shall pay its debt and Abaddon will give back that which was committed into it, that I may render unto every man according to his works and according to the fruit of their imaginations, until I judge between the soul and the flesh. And the world shall rest, and death shell be quenched, and Sheol shall shut its mouth. And the earth shall not be without birth, neither barren for them that dwell therein; and none shall be polluted that hath been justified in Me. And there shall be another earth and anther heaven, even an everlasting habitation.[102]

One of the most important questions, which we need to ask, is what was the relationship between the two aeons in the Rabbinico-Jewish eschatology? To answer this question, we need to examine the exact

---

[101] Ibid., 135-151.
[102] Ibid., 140.

understanding of the Rabbis about the nature of the concept. They viewed
the nature of the two aeons as three-dimensional. First dimension is the
spatial one, namely this age and the age to come have spatial relation.
According to Jewish understanding there were two worlds, namely
heavenly one that is the dwelling place of God and the earthly one the
dwelling place of the humans. They sharply contrasted these two
spheres.[103] Their temporal element was inadequate since the age to come
has always existed above this age, or with the other words the 'olam ha-ba'
has been always there in heaven. That can be seen in several Apocalyptic
passages.

> And he said unto me
> He proclaims unto thee peace in the name of the world
>   to come.
> For from hence has proceeded peace since the creation
>   of the world.
> And so shall it be forever and forever and ever.[104]

> And there I saw another vision, the dwelling places of
>   the holy,
> And the resting-places of the righteous.
> Here mine eyes saw their dwelling places with his
>   righteous angels,
> And their resting places with the holy.[105]

Furthermore, the 'ha olam ha-ba' is experienced by the person at
the time of death and is introduced by the judgment of the soul. That is
clearly seen in the passage from the rabbinical literature concerning R.
Johanan b. Zakkai:

---

[103] Gerald F. Hawthorne and Ralph P. Martin, eds. *Dictionary of Paul and His Letters*, s.v. "Apocalypticism," by D. E. Aune.

[104] 1 Enoch 71:15, quoted in W. D. Davies, 315.

[105] 1 Enoch 39:4, quoted in Ibid.

When R. Johannan b. Zakkai was ill, his disciples went in to visit him. On beholding them, he began to weep. His disciples said to him, 'O lamp of Israel, right hand pillar [1 Kings 7:21], mighty hammer, wherefore dost thou weep?' He replied to them, 'If I was being led into the presence of a human king, who to-day is here and to-morrow in the grave, whose anger, if he were wrathful against us, would not be eternal, whose imprisonment, if he imprisoned me, would not be everlasting, whose death sentence, if he condemned me to death, would not be for ever, and whom I could appease with words and bribe with money-even then I would weep; but now, when I am being led into the presence of the king of kings, the Holy One, blessed by He, who lives and endures for all eternity, whose anger, if He be wrathful against me, is eternal, whose imprisonment, if He imprisoned me, would be everlasting, whose sentence, if He condemned me to death, would be for ever, and whom I cannot appease with words or bribe with money-nay, more, when before me lie two ways, one towards the Garden of Eden and the other towards Gehinnom, and I know not towards which I am to be led-shall I not weep?' They said to him, 'Our master, bless us!' He said to them, 'May it be His will that the fear of heaven be upon you [as great] as the fear of flesh and blood.' His disciples exclaimed, 'Only as great!' He replied, 'Would that it be [as great]; for know, that when a man intends to commit a transgression, he says, 'I hope nobody will see me.'[106]

Second dimension of the two aeons is a temporal one. This age is now and the age to come is coming in the future "after the Messianic Age

---

[106] B. Ber.28b, quoted in Ibid., 315, 316.

and the general resurrection."[107] We will not offer a particular passage because as Davies says "there are plenty of them." And the third dimension is a qualitative one. It follows the same characteristics as those we already mentioned in our previous discussion of Apocalyptic eschatology. The particular passage which can be considered is the one concerning the death of R. Johanan b. Zakkai, which has been previously quoted. Thus, we can sum up the relationship between the two aeons in their three dimensions in the following way: the age to come, which is imperishable and eternal, is at the present time parallel to this age, which is temporary and perishable, and at the time of the final consummation it is replacing this age or overcoming it. Furthermore, we have the two aeons with their three-dimensional structure which overlaps at one point, namely they overlap at the time of man's death. One further conclusion could be served on the basis of our previously presented discussion and it is well presented by Strack-Billerbeck.

> ...Yet the striking phenomenon that the Rabbinic teachers have used the expression *ha-olam ha-ba* to designate both the heavenly world of the souls and also the future Age of Consummation would have made it clear to us, as it were, that the heavenly Aeon of the Souls and the future Aeon of consummation of earth where regarded as one and the same great *olam ha-ba*. This great *olam ha-ba* at preset had its place in heaven (1 Enoch 71:14ff) ... into it the souls of the righteous entered at the hour of death for a preliminary blessedness. That is their first phase in which it severs as the world of the souls until it enters thorough the resurrection of the dead into its second phase in order now to become the early sphere of the Aeon of full blessedness.[108]

---

[107] Ibid., 316.

[108]H. L. Strack and Billerbeck, vol. IV, pp. 819f, quoted in W. D. Davies, 316, 317.

In summary, the First Century Rabbinico-Jewish eschatology overtook the concept of the two aeons and used it for constructing of its own framework. In general the three-dimensional structure of the concept is well preserved. The contrast between the two aeons is kept but also the point of overlapping between the two aeons is plainly shown by the Rabbinic writings. That understanding of the concept of the two aeons prepared the ground for New Testament eschatology.

B. NEW TESTAMENT ESCHATOLOGY

Turning to the New Testament eschatology we will attempt to construct the understanding of the two aeons in the New Testament writings. We will conduct that research by examining Jesus' teaching as found in the Gospels, view points of the Gospel writers, and Paul's understanding of the matter.

1. Jesus' Apocalyptic framework

Few methods are recognized in respect of scholarly outlook of Jesus' Apocalyptic framework of his teaching. Some scholars as J. Weiss and A. Schweitzer argued that Jesus' teaching was thoroughly Apocalyptic but basically wrong in relation to the age to come. He expected the new age to come during his ministry but it did not come. Hence, he tried to inaugurate it through his death but he mistakenly died without any success. Those scholars called their understanding "consistent eschatology." Others as R. Bultmann defended Jesus' Apocalyptic framework through the means of existentialism. He applied his demythologizing program in the interpretation of Jesus' teaching with the purpose to show its existentialist's nature, namely that Jesus' Apocalyptic teaching tried to help man to open themselves toward God's future. Still others as C. H. Dodd viewed Jesus' Apocalyptic framework of his teaching through the prism of realized eschatology. In other words, they tried to show that all the Old Testament prophesies were fulfilled in the ministry of Jesus and God's kingdom was completely established. All the future elements of Jesus' teaching were only a creation of the early church. And even others as Marcus J. Borg argue against Apocalyptic framework of Jesus' teaching. He maintains that Jesus spoke about the kingdom of God in mystical fashion. The kingdom is neither here and now, nor is it on ahead, but it is "up there." "The kingdom already exists in a realm transcending time."[109] However, some conservative scholars as G. E. Ladd, E. E. Ellis, and I. H. Marshall found

---

[109] Reginald H. Fuller, "Jesus, Paul and Apocalyptic," *Anglican Theological Review 71* (Spring 1989): 137.

the appropriate balance in understanding Jesus' Apocalyptic framework. Jesus spoke about the present reality of the kingdom of God as well as he showed its future aspect. "The kingdom was paradoxically 'present' and 'still to come.'"[110]

> For Jesus, the kingdom of God, the eschatological establishment of God's kingly rule, was due to come in is fullness soon. And when it came, after the judgment and their resurrection, the world would be new, the powers of evil eliminated, and the will of God accomplished perfectly. If Jesus spoke of the kingdom as already present, that was because, in his eyes, the powers of the coming age had, in his person and ministry, already begun to invade and thus transform the here and now: the night was giving way to the light of a new day.[111]

Dale C. Allison's presentation of Jesus' view of the kingdom of God is also well balanced with the tension between "already" and "not yet."

> Jesus taught that the Evil One was still in control of this present world, but that in some sense he was already defeated. Jesus taught that with his own coming, judgment on the world had come, but that nevertheless a future judgment was to be expected (Jn 12:31; 16:11). He taught that final vindication for his followers would be in eternity, but that even in this life they would also be well compensated for any sacrifices they were being asked to make (M 10:29-

---

[110] M. J. Borg, *Jesus: Conflict, Holiness and Politics in the Teachings of Jesus* (SBEC 5: New York/Toronto: Mellen, 1984), quoted in Joel B. Green and Scot McKnight, eds. *Dictionary of Jesus and the Gospels* (Leicester, England: Inter - Varsity Press, 1992), s.v. "Apocalyptic Teaching," by T. J. Geddet.

[111] Dale C. Allison, *The End of The Ages Has Come: An Early Interpretation of the Passion and Resurrection of Jesus* (Edinburgh: T. and T. Clark, 1985), 114.

30). He taught that final salvation was still awaited (Mt 24:13), yet that salvation was already available to those who followed him (Lk 19:9).[112]

In comparison with the first century Rabbinico-Jewish eschatology we can clearly see that Jesus' Apocalyptic framework was not a complete blueprint of the Rabbis understanding of the two aeons concept. However, it took over some of its features. Jesus viewed the history as divided in two, namely two ages. And further, Jesus preserved the three-dimensional nature of the two ages as expressed both by the Apocalyptists and by the Rabbis, namely the spatial, the temporal, and the qualitative. Nevertheless, he modified the concept by softening the contrast between the two aeons, presenting the new aeon as inaugurated in his ministry. Thus, at that very point, the two aeons clearly overlapped. The ground for that strong overlapping of the two ages has been already established, as we saw, in the Rabbinico-Jewish eschatology, even though the point of that overlapping was completely different. Moreover, Jesus introduced a new dimension never seen before him, namely the "already" and "not yet." In his ministry Jesus underlined the "already" present new aeon, but he also spoke about it's "not yet" aspect. Thus, he saw in his coming and ministry as the inauguration of the kingdom of God and its powerful advancing, but he saw as well its full future consummation in the Day of the Lord (e.g., Lk 21:34-36). Let us turn now to the Gospel writers and see whether they followed the same moderate Apocalyptic framework of Jesus.

2. Gospels' Apocalyptic framework

We will examine in this section all four Gospel's writers in respect to their understanding of the two aeons concept. We will not restrict our examination only to the four Gospels but we will also include Acts and Revelation.

---

[112] Joel B. Green and Scot McKnight, eds. *Dictionary of Jesus and the Gospels*, s.v. "Apocalyptic Teaching," by T. J. Geddet.

a) Mark

The emphasis of Mark's Gospel in general is on radical discipleship. He expresses it through the modified Apocalyptic framework of the two aeons concept. Hence, we can easily discern how the two ages overlap in Mark. Mark's prophecies about the future are bound together with the present call for discipleship. The latter are expressed firmly in the light of the Apocalyptic promises (cf.8:31- 9:1; 10:17-31).[113] Thus Mark views Jesus' death and resurrection as the means for establishing a new community of God's people. However, that community has been already called before Jesus' death took place. Jesus' pupils were summoned for a life of radical discipleship. That included following of the steps of their teacher and Lord, sufferings and persecutions, in order to inherit the glorious Kingdom in the coming age. Thus, through this presentation Mark tries to balance the view of his readers so that they would not only think about the Christian life looking through the prism of the glory and honor of the imminent-coming End, but also to look at the preceding hard time of suffering which is expected of them. [114]

Furthermore, one of the clearest pictures of Mark's Apocalyptic framework is his "Apocalyptic discourse" in chapter 13. Although it does not carry many of the features of the Apocalyptic literature it is closely related to it.[115] Moreover, we can recognize there the stamp of the concept of the two aeons.

> Mark 13 ... clearly reflects a view of history/eschatology in which a present age of crisis

---

[113] Ibid.

[114] Morna D. Hooker, *The Gospel According to Saint Mark*, Black's New Testament Commentary, ed. Henry Chadwick (Peabody, Massachusetts: Hendrickson Publishers, 1991), 19-26.

[115] Gerald F. Hawthorne and Ralph P. Martin, eds. *Dictionary of Paul and His Letters* (Leicester, England: Inter - Varsity Press, 1993), s.v. "Apcalyptic," by D. C. Allison, Jr.

> and persecution will give way to a future age in which
> God exercises judgment on his enemies and vindicates
> and rewards his elect. Moreover, it contains
> eschatological prediction and warns the elect of
> impending deceptions and disasters.[116]

We can conclude that within his unique emphasis Mark follows the
modified structure of Jesus' Apocalyptic framework.

b) Matthew

Reading Matthew's Gospel we clearly see the presence of the
Apocalyptic elements. Moreover, his Apocalyptic discourse is closely
linked with the Apocalyptic discourse of Mark. The same kind of emphasis
is placed on discipleship (24:43-44, 45-51; 24:1-13, 14-30, 31-46). The
difference from Mark is that Matthew has a negative perspective versus the
positive of Mark. In other words, Mark speaks about the blessings which
are coming for those who are following Jesus; Matthew speaks about the
judgment about those who refuse to follow his master. Matthew as well
makes some further emphasis on the inauguration of the new age by
presenting some clear Apocalyptic signs which accompanied the
resurrection of Christ, such as earthquake, angelic presence, and fear for
those who have seen it.[117] Thus Dale C. Allison has right to argue that "in
Matthew, ... this age and the age to come overlap. Although the
consummation lies ahead, although this age is still full of tribulation, and
although the Christian casts his hope upon the future coming of the Son of
man, saints have already been raised, the Son of man has already been
enthroned in the heavenly places, and the resurrected Jesus is ever present
with his followers (28:20)."[118] Thus we can conclude that Matthew's

---

[116] Joel B. Green and Scot McKnight, eds. *Dictionary of Jesus and the
Gospels,* s.v. "Apocalyptic Teaching," by T. J. Geddet.

[117] Ibid.

[118] Dale C. Allison, *The End of The Ages Has Come,* 49, 50.

Apocalyptic framework is established upon that of his teacher following the same structure of "already" and "not yet."

c) Luke

Luke as well as other evangelists uses some Apocalyptic elements in his writings. Thus, in his so-called Q Apocalypse, Luke parallels the Apocalyptic discourses of Mark 13 and Matthew 24. However, some scholars argue that Luke diminishes the "not yet" aspect in his Apocalyptic framework. Even though in some aspects Luke emphasizes the "already" it is not reasonable to argue that he does not present the "not yet" aspect. For example, both in his gospel and in Acts, Luke stresses on the subject of the future return of Christ.

> H. Conzelmann underestimated Luke's interest in futurist eschatology. A. J. Mattill, in responding to Conzelmann, seems to have underestimated the realized elements. The kingdom is portrayed in Luke as already and not yet, just as it is in the other Gospels, even though differences in emphasis can be detected.[119]

Hence, I. Howard Marshall could relate Luke's eschatological framework to the Apocalyptic eschatology in the following way: "the decisive eschatological event had taken place in the ministry of Jesus; the eschatological content of the original Apocalyptic tradition was seen to be fulfilled in Jesus, and the remaining Apocalyptic imagery was reserved for fulfillment in the distant future."[120] Furthermore, Marshall concludes about Luke's presentation of Jesus' teaching about the kingdom of God.

---

[119] Joel B. Green and Scot McKnight, eds. *Dictionary of Jesus and the Gospels*, s.v. "Apocalyptic Teaching," by T. J. Geddet.

[120] I. Haward Marshall, *Luke-Historian and Theologian* (London: The Paternoster Press, 1970), 82.

> It has emerged that in the Gospel of Luke the teaching of Jesus regarding the presence and the future coming of the kingdom is faithfully reproduced. While Luke retains the hope of the future coming of the kingdom, he also stresses the presence of the kingdom as a reality in the ministry of Jesus.[121]

Hence, the two eschatological dimensions in the framework of Luke's gospel are thoroughly clear, the kingdom of God is "already" in Jesus' ministry but "not yet" completely consumed. In Acts of the Apostles, Luke also keeps the tension between "already" and "not yet" alive. He plainly expresses the reality of the new age in all the miracles which are following the disciples of Jesus and at the same time speaks clearly about the future second coming of their teacher. Thus, we conclude that Luke is faithful to the Apocalyptic framework of his teacher and follows it consistently even though with his own emphatic uniqueness.

d) John

John compared to the other three evangelists is unique in his presentation of the gospel and the usage of the Apocalyptic framework of Jesus. He stresses the "already" aspect of that framework. John presents, for example, the judgement as already executed in Jesus' ministry toward those who have rejected him (3:18) and also the resurrection for those who believed in him (5:24-25). Satan is depicted as defeated in the ministry of Jesus. The evangelist also underlines the notion that after the resurrection, Jesus will still be present in the lives of his disciples through his Spirit (cf. Jn 20:22). Hence some scholars have been led to argue that the "not yet" aspect disappears from John. However, this is not a complete understanding of John's gospel. The evangelist presents the stories in his gospel holding "one eye on the historical events of Jesus' life and death, and another on

---

[121] Ibid., 136.

the final eschatological events for which Jesus is preparing. It is John's way of presenting the already/not yet paradox."[122]

In his Apocalypse, however, John balances the eschatological perspective of the two aeons concept. He stresses on both the present aeon and the aeon to come. Thus, the scenario of the book appears usual for Apocalyptic eschatology, namely "that it culminates in the end of this world and the judgement of the dead."[123] But also has clearly undergone the changes of the Christian understanding of the two aeons, namely that the new aeon has already been inaugurated in Jesus' death and resurrection. Hence, John can encourage his readers through the perspective that "the crucial act of deliverance has already taken place with the death and resurrection of Jesus."[124]   However, he does not erase the future aeon but places it in the immanent mode next to the present one. Thus, we have the balance "the death of Jesus marks a veritable D-day in the eschatological timetable, but the final judgment is yet to come."[125] We clearly see in John's writings that the Apocalyptic framework of Jesus is well preserved and expressed.

3. Paul's Apocalyptic framework

Now turning to Paul's understanding and use of the concept of the two aeons in his writings we need to remember the fact that as a Rabbinic pupil Paul was entirely exposed to the previously presented Rabbinico-Apoclyptic relationship between the two aeons. Hence, Paul knew and believed the three-dimensional nature of this age and the age to come. He expected the age to come to arrive in the future and also, he expected to enter it at his death. We need to examine, however, whether after his

---

[122] Joel B. Green and Scot McKnight, eds. *Dictionary of Jesus and the Gospels*, s.v. "Apocalyptic Teaching," by T. J. Geddet.

[123] John J. Collins, *The Apocalyptic Imagination: An Introduction to Jewish Apocalyptic Literature* (Grand Rapids, Michigan: William B. Eerdmans Publishing Company, 1984), 269.

[124] Ibid., 278.

[125] Ibid., 269-278.

conversion to Christianity, his understanding of the two aeons concept had experienced any changes.

In general scholars agree that the main change in Paul's view of the two aeons appeared because of the event of Jesus' resurrection. It became for Paul the point of inauguration of the age to come in this age. Hence, the age to come in its three dimensions has been inaugurated in the present age through the event of Jesus' resurrection. However, the scholars divide on what extent Paul understood the establishment and the interaction of the age to come within the present age. Some as Davies and Dodd would argue that Paul viewed the presence of the age to come in the present age as total and complete. There would be no further changes of the condition of the believers. They have been already resurrected with Christ and they only expect to be finally revealed as such. "This means that Christians are already partakers in the Age to come 'in Christ' and that future events can only make this fact explicit."[126] Dodd even dares to say that there is no future dimension of the age to come. According to him the futurist element in the thought of Jesus and Paul is just an Apocalyptic language which is used symbolically. Thus, there will be no Second Coming of Jesus and there will be no future point of complete consummation of the Kingdom of God.[127] On the other hand, some as J. Christiaan Beker argue that Paul's thought has been completely absorbed by the future dimension of the age to come.[128]

Beker argues that "Paul's 'Apocalyptic structure of thought' forms the consistent and indispensable 'center' of his thought."[129] This understanding is also supported by the scholars as Albert Schweitzer, Johannes Weiss, Ernst Kasemann and Klaus Koch.[130] However, Vincent

---

[126] W. D. Davies, 319.

[127] Dodd, *The Parables of the Kindom*, p. 104f, 108, quoted in W. D. Davies, 319, 320.

[128] J. Christiaan Beker, *Paul's Apocalyptic Gospel: The Coming Triumph of God*, 76.

[129] J. Christiaan Beker, *Paul the Apostle: The Triumph of God in Life and Thought* (Philadelphia: Fortress, 1970), 16, 135, quoted in Vincent P. Branick "Apocalyptic Paul?" *Catholic Biblical Quarterly 47:664-675* (October 1985): 664.

[130] Ibid., 664.

P. Branick critiques Beker that he is "inconsistent" in presenting Paul's Apocalyptic framework.[131]

Beker defines three main traits of the Apocalyptic literature: "(1) historical dualism, (2) universal cosmic expectation, and (3) the imminent end of the world."[132] These three characteristics find their full resolution in the Apocalyptic concept of physical and spiritual salvation of the cosmos in general and to mankind in particular. Salvation is anticipated in the present age and fully consumed in the age to come. Beker sees these primary Apocalyptic features as the foundation of Paul's theology. Paul's clearly Apocalyptic emphasis rests on the future full realization of salvation as the experience of the bodily resurrection of believers and transformation of the world. However, according to Beker, Paul does not narrow his view only on the future age but contrary to the traditional Apocalyptic he sees the future age as already inaugurated in the resurrection of Christ. This is expressed by the apostle with the expression as 'the first fruits,' and 'down payment,' referring to the experience of the future age in the present one by the believers. Thus, "Paul's Apocalyptic exhibits the paradoxical tension of the 'already' and the 'not yet." Beker argues that Paul modifies Jewish Apocalyptic understanding of the two-age concept in two directions, namely softening it and intensifying it.

First, Paul sees the old history of Israel as not in such dark colors as the Apocalyptists did because of the promises of God which expected fulfillment in the age to come. Thus, he softens the contrast between the two ages by acknowledging the important place of Israel's history in God's plan and also its "temporary splendor," (2 Cor 3:7-11)."[133] Paul also softens the contrast between the two aeons by introducing the inauguration of the age to come in this age by the event of Christ. Already the powers of the new age are working in those who are in Christ, the Spirit of God enables them to experience the blessings of the new age while living in the present one. Second, Paul intensifies the contrast between the two ages. The powers of the age to come became active in this age. Thus, the powers of life from the age to come are confronted with the powers of death from this

---

[131] Ibid.

[132] Vincent P. Branick, 665.

[133] J. Christiaan Beker, *Paul's Apocalyptic Gospel: The Coming Triumph of God*, 40.

age. The contrast is complete, a crisis starts. This is the crisis for those who are living in this world of death clothed with the powers of life from the new age. The Church, the body of believers, is in a position of war against the world, "because the cross of Christ represents God's radical 'No' to the value structures of our present world. For the powers of this age have not only crucified Christ (1 Cor 2:8) but continue to crucify those who belong to Christ (2Cor 4:7-12)."[134]

Beker sharply criticizes all the non-Apocalyptic approaches to Paul. He places under this category three such theories: "realized eschatology, existentialist analysis of the gospel, and the scheme of salvation-history."[135] Thus, he criticizes scholars as C. H. Dodd and Rudolf Bultmann because of their transferring of the Apocalyptic into "a radical ethic."[136] Beker completely rejects their existentialists' views as abstracting Paul's theology from its Apocalyptic matrix. Actually, Paul's theology cannot be understood out of its Apocalyptic framework. However, according to Branick, Beker has gone into the extreme of criticizing those who disregard the Apocalyptic framework of Paul. He views some of the biblical authors also abandoning the Apocalyptic perspective, namely Luke in Acts and John in his gospel.[137] Moreover, he stays against the claim of Beker that "Christian ethical life is distorted in Colossians and Ephesians because of the insistence of these writings on a realized resurrection (Col 2:12; Eph 2:4-6) and a premature spiritual perfection."[138] It should be underlined, however, that in agreement with Beker, Branick criticizes the existentialists.

---

[134] Ibid., 41.

[135] Ibid., 65.

[136] "Albert Schweitzer thus transpierced Apocalyptic into 'reverence for life.' Robert Jewett interprets the Apocalyptic command to vigilance in terms of the need to be prepared for the unexpected, 'a watchful expectancy for the Abba's work and will,' a willingness 'to taste his grace in the new dawn of every day." Vincent P. Branick, 667.

[137] In his intention to balance the extreme futuristic-Apocalyptic understanding of Beker Branick has gone too far in striping Acts and John's gospel from the futuristic elements of their Apocalyptic framework which we presented before. (See Luke and John sections from Gospels' Apocalyptic framework.)

[138] Vincent P. Branick, 675.

> Attempts of existential theology to translate the images into ethical and attitudinal challenge including challenges of public and cosmic proportions-do in fact explore the difference between symbol and mystery. These attempts from the very lifeblood of theology as something other than biblicism.[139]

Another group of scholars, whose representatives are Vincent Branick and Aune,[140] argue about the balance in Paul's understanding of the present and future temporal dimensions of the age to come. Aune sees that there is a balance between the two dimensions of the two-aeon concept even in the Apocalyptic literature in general and in the Second Temple Judaism in particular.

> This spatial dualism (heaven as the dwelling place of God and his angels; earth as the dwelling place of humanity) coincided with temporal or eschatological dualism in the sense that the kingdom of God, or the age to come, was a heavenly reality which would eventually displace the earthly reality of the present evil age.[141]

He affirms that this balance extends to the Pauline view also. Thus, Paul accommodated the same understanding in general, viewing the cosmos as divided in two main realms, heaven and earth (1 Cor 8:5; 15:47-50; Col 1:16, 20; Eph 1:10; 3:16). Paul as an Apocalyptists saw the heaven as the dwelling place of God and angels, and also according to the Christian tradition based upon Ps 110:1, Jesus as sitting at the right hand of God (Rom 1:18; 10:6; Gal 1:8; Eph 6:9; Rom 8:35; Col 3:1).[142]

---

[139] Ibid.

[140] Gerald F. Hawthorne and Ralph P. Martin, eds. *Dictionary of Paul and His Letters*, s.v. "Apocalypticism," by D. E. Aune.

[141] Ibid., 32.

[142] Ibid.

Part II. Development of the Two Aeons Concept in First Century Judaism and Biblical Literature

Branick defines Apocalyptic as "a hermeneutic key to Paul." He views some important parts of Paul's theology through the perspective of the Apocalyptic outlook. Hence the "flesh" and "spirit" concepts are not developed on the basis of Gnostic's understanding of the body but are purely seen as "cosmic dimensions," "Apocalyptic aeons in which humanity lives and walks."[143] Furthermore, Paul's Apocalyptic hermeneutic allows us to see the Apostle's presentation of salvation not only as a personal matter but also as embracing the whole of the universe (heaven and earth, 2 Cor.5:17). And from this perspective the problem of sin is not related only to the individual but also to the whole universe. As in the Apocalyptic literature Paul defines the sin not primary as "ethical defect" but as "a cosmic force." In agreement with Apocalyptists, Paul underlines the future aspect of the age to come. Moreover, Branick sees the development of Paul's realized eschatology in Paul's historical dualistic thought. According to him, Paul views history in two parts, namely two aeons. Those are expressed by the apostle with phrases such as "before faith" and "now" (Gal 3:23-29); "being a child" and "the fullness" (Gal 4:1-7). Furthermore, he finds throughout Pauline corpus clear references to the realized eschatology. As in Rom 6:4 the newness of life is discussed next to the future resurrection of the body (Rom 6:5). In 2 Cor 4:16 Paul speaks about the inner transformation of self, which echoes the Jeremiah's concept of establishing of the new covenant (2 Cor 3:3). Paul's language of abundance in a present time versus the condition of the believers "before faith" plainly presents Paul's understanding of the present time as one of eschatological fullness. Moreover, as Fredrich Hauch says "this language of abundance speaks of a fullness present and proclaimed in the age of salvation as compared with the old aeon."[144] The language "in Christ"[145]

---

[143] Vincent P. Branick, 666.

[144] Friedrich Hauch, "perisseuo," TDNT 6 (1968) 59, quoted in Ibid., 672.

[145] "The eschatological transformation of the individual arises from union with and participation in Christ: hence, Paul's characteristic use of his syn-verbs, referring to a joint activity involving Christ and the Christian. Some of these refer to the future (*syzao*, Rom 6:8; *syndoxazo*, Rom 8:17); others clearly refer to the present (*systauroo*, Rom 6:6; Gal 2:19; *synthapto*, Rom 6:4; *sympascho*, Rom 8:17; and *symmorphizo*, Phil 3:10)." Ibid., 672.

leads to understand that "the new eschatological aeon has begun."[146] Thus, for Branick the concept of "already" and "not yet" does not only present the "clash of the Apocalyptic aeons," but also the "progressive transformation" of Christians in terms of the "intensification of life ('from life to life," 2 Cor 2:16) and intensification of glory ('from glory to glory,' 2 Cor 3:18)."[147]

Branick criticizes Beker that he excluded the realized eschatological part of Paul's theology from his observations. One of the features of this part of Paul's theology is the tension between the "already" and "not yet." Beker recognizes that that is a new feature of Paul's Apocalyptic thinking which differs from the traditional apocalyptism. Thus, Branick admits that Beker speaks about the "already" part of Paul's theology but he argues that it is not enough. He finds Beker's biggest fault in incapability in general to see the eschatological diversity of the NT and in particular to allow the concept of "already" to stay next to the concept of "not yet."[148]

> The Apocalyptic perspective does not really help insofar as it presents the death and resurrection of Christ as only the promise of future rescue. In this case justification and salvation have not rally taken place for humanity as a whole. The 'already' has collapsed. Jesus' resurrection becomes a great thing for him, but only a carrot held out for us.
>
> The Ephesians/Johannine approach is to see the 'already' as a spiritual realization of the eschaton in the life of the believer. In this way Ephesians can speak of Christians as already raised up and given a place in the heavens. 'While we were dead in our sins, God brought us to life with Christ – by grace we are saved – and raised us and seated us in the heavens in Christ Jesus' (Eph 2:5-6). Similarly in

---

[146] Ibid.

[147] Ibid., 674.

[148] Vincent P. Branick, 672-675.

> John, Jesus now grants eternal life to the one 'who hears my word and has faith in him who sent me' (John 5:24). As Jesus tells Martha, 'I am the resurrection and the life… whoever is alive and believes in me will never die.' (John 11:25-26).
>
> Colossians, on which Ephesians appears to have a direct literary dependence, likewise insists on a realized eschatology. 'In baptism you were buried with him, in whom you were also raised through faith in the power of God which raised him from the dead' (2:12). Scholarship disputes the authenticity expression of realized eschatology in Colossians, however, Beker does not consider even the possibility of its authenticity, but rather finds it a clear expression of the later refection of Pauline Apocalyptic, an expression of a distortion of Christian ethical life." [149]

However, Beker clearly recognizes the tension of "already" and "not yet" as presented in Ephesians in the "cosmic dimension of the historical suffering of the church."[150] Branick affirms Beker's understanding of the Paul's Apocalyptic framework but does not agree with Beker's rigid applying of this framework with stubborn consistency throughout Pauline corpus. He contrary to Beker does not exclude the realized eschatology as part of Paul's theological thought. Thus, he puts realized and future eschatology next to the other even in the letters which are under question of their authenticity. He claims that although Colossians "affirms the realized 'resurrection' of the Christian (2:12)… it also proclaims the future parousia" [151](Col 3:3-4).

---

[149] Vincent P. Branick, 672.

[150] J. Christiaan Beker, *Paul's Apocalyptic Gospel: The Coming Triumph of God*, 41.

[151] Vincent P. Branick, 675.

Aune defines Paul's eschatology as continuation of "the temporal dualistic thought of Jewish Apocalypticism."[152] As such, Paul views the time divided in two ages, the present age and the age to come. (Gal 1:4; Rom.8:18; 1 Cor 1:26; Eph 5:16) According to Aune, however, Paul "considerably modified" Apocalyptists' temporal dualism of the two aeons in the sense that he saw this age and the age to come not in such a contrast as they presented it. He believed that his generation was living in the "end of the ages (1 Cor 10:11)," meaning that the two aeons clashed in the death and the resurrection of Jesus. The latter appears for Paul to be the crucial event, which not only separates the two aeons but also by which the new aeon is inaugurated.   Thus, those who are in Jesus "share in the salvific benefits of the age to come (Gal 1:4; 2 Cor 5:17)."[153]   Aune argues, however, that "Paul did not explicitly use the phrase 'the age to come." Nevertheless, he says that in 2 Cor 5:17 and Gal 6:15 he speaks about the "new creation," phrase used in the Apocalyptic literature sometimes as a substitution for the age to come. This claim of Aune could be objected because we have in Eph 1:21 clear expression of the whole phrase "this age and the age to come," "*aiōni toutō ... kai en tō mellonti.*" Perhaps the author does not consider Ephesians as Pauline but nevertheless, his usage of references from the letter shows otherwise.

Moreover, Aune argues that "the basic salvation-history framework of Paul's thought incorporates within it the Apocalyptic notion of the two successive ages."[154] He provides supportive arguments from Paul's dividing of history in the realms of Adam and Christ in Rom 5:12-21. Furthermore, Paul viewed the Christian life as shaped in the tension of "already and not yet." Thus, he was arguing through the grammatical categories of indicative and imperative such as in Gal 5:25. "If we live [indicative] in the Spirit, let us also walk [imperative] in the Spirit." Hence, the Christians should in daily obedience to the Lord reject the temptations of the world and the flesh.

Therefore, we can conclude that Paul followed the Apocalyptic framework of Jesus as far as the other New Testament writers followed it.

---

[152] Gerald F. Hawthorne and Ralph P. Martin, eds. *Dictionary of Paul and His Letters*, s.v. "Apocalypticism," by D. E. Aune.

[153] Ibid.

[154] Ibid.

He viewed the history as divided in two, this age and the age to come.
Moreover, the three dimensions of the ages were preserved by the apostle.
The same new element was introduced in the old Apocalyptic concept of
the two aeons, namely that of the "already" and "not yet." In the
resurrection of Jesus, the new aeon has been inaugurated. Thus, for those
who are in Christ the new age has already started but it has not yet been
completely fulfilled. On the basis of that new element in the concept, Paul,
as well as Jesus, softened the contrast between the two ages.

E. CONCLUSION

Looking on the concept of the two aeons in the first century
Rabbinc-Judaism we reached the conclusion that it found its place firmly
in Jewish eschatology. However, the concept has experienced some
modifications. The contrast between the two aeons and their three
dimensions were clearly defined, but also the point of overlapping between
them was established. That was at the time of one's death. Thus, that has
softened a bit the formal contrast between the two ages presented by the
Apocalytists. Proceeding further with analyzing the New Testament
against this background we found out that Jesus in general, the evangelists
and Paul in particular, have adapted what already long ago existed - the
concept of the two aeons. However, they once again modified it in regard
to the relationship between the two aeons. The two aeons are not anymore
completely separated, whether in space, time or quality. The new aeon has
already been inaugurated in the present aeon through the event of Christ.
The new dimension has been established, namely the "already" and "not
yet." Hence, the experience of the future aeon is available to those who are
living in Christ.

CONCLUSION

In the present research project, we overtook the task to analyze the origins and development of the doctrine of the two aeons. We followed two general lines of investigation, namely in the prophetic and Apocalyptic eschatology on one hand, and in the New Testament on the other hand, against the background of the First Century Rabbinical Judaism. We would attempt now to state clearly the conclusions reached throughout our research.

First, throughout our examination of the prophetic and Apocalyptic eschatology we underlined the concept of the two aeons as clearly present in them. Both prophets and Apocalyptists viewed the deep gap between the two aeons. Although, the prophets overcome in a sense the latter by making an analogy between God's saving acts in the formal history of Israel and his deeds of inaugurating the new age; and the Apocalypitists presented the gap as completely separating the two ages. Moreover, both prophets and Apocalyptists viewed the newness of the new age and its blessings and the corruption of the present age. Thus, we stressed the fact that the concept of the two aeons established one of the strongest lines of continuity between prophetic and Apocalyptic traditions in general and their eschatology in particular. However, we plainly detected the fact that the concept did not originate from them. The original roots of the concept are found in the ancient Near-East mythology, namely Canaan and Babylonian primitive traditions and Iranian-Babylonian syncretism. Moreover, it is clear that the Apocalyptists developed the concept of the two aeons which they took over from the prophets and from ancient Near-East mythology. The Prophets did not have a clear picture of the nature of the two aeons. On the other hand, the Apocalyptists viewed the two aeons as consisting of three-dimensions, namely spatial, temporal, and qualitative. Moreover, they extended their scope on God's work in the new age from nationalistic to universalistic. God is not only working with Israel but also with the rest of the world. And finally, their differentiation of the two aeons was stronger than that of the prophets.

Second, with such an understanding of the origins and development of the concept in the prophets and Apocalyptists we turned to examining the Rabbinic-Judaism in the First Century after Christ and New Testament literature. Thus, our research showed that the concept of the two aeons has been adapted and modified by the First Century Rabbis. They preserved the three dimensions of the two aeons and also pointed to a clear overlapping place between them. That has softened a bit the formal contrast between the two ages presented by the apocalytists. On the other hand, within such an environment Jesus, the Gospel writers, and Paul felt obligated to present their eschatology within the already existing framework of the two aeons. They used the general characteristic of the concept, the three-dimensional nature of the present and the future age. Moreover, they used some elements from the Apocalyptic understanding such as the universalistic nature of God's acts in the future age. However, they introduced some purely new characteristics of the concept under discussion which underlined the foundation of Christian movement, namely the ministry, the death, and the resurrection of Christ. That new characteristic of the concept was based on the fact that they viewed the inauguration of the future aeon in the present aeon through the event of Christ. Thus, the future aeon has entered the present aeon preserving its three-dimensional nature. The eternal age to come has begun and the everlasting world above has descended in the present temporary and perishable age here and now for those who are in Christ. Nevertheless, the future aspect and the aeon to come have been plainly preserved. The final consummation of the age to come has not yet taken place. The heavenly world has not yet fully descended on earth. Those are the events which are expected within the future, although they are already anticipated by the believers. Even though the formal contrast between the two aeons, which the Apocalyptists developed, was partly overcome, there was still contrast between the present and the future aeon and it is experienced by those who are part of the future aeon but still living in the present one; that contrast is expressed in the tension between "already" and "not yet." The latter is the new characteristic introduced and developed by Jesus and the New Testament authors.

Therefore, with our introductory perspective we may state that: we as Christians need to manage thoroughly the existing developed understanding of the two aeons in order to have a proper ground for understanding of Christian faith and theology. Moreover, through the perspective of the two aeons we have the right answer for the world which is preoccupied with the concerns about the future. The 21st Century man can enter the future age and become a part of the future humanity and world by the one and only way, namely, to believe in Jesus Christ, who brought the future age into the present one through his ministry, death, and resurrection and made it available to all who believe and come to him in repentance.

BIBLIOGRAPHY

Allison, Dale C. *The End of The Ages Has Come: An Early Interpretation of the Passion and Resurrection of Jesus.* Edinburgh: T. and T. Clark, 1985.

Armerding, Carl E. "Prophecy in the Old Testament." in *Handbook of Biblical Prophecy*, eds. Carl E. Armerding and W. Ward Gasque. Grand Rapids, Michigan: Baker Book House, 1977.

Beker, J. Christiaan *Paul's Apcalyptic Gospel: The Coming Triumph of God.* Philadelphia: Fortress Press, 1982.

________. *Paul the Apostle: The Triumph of God in Life and Thought* (Philadelphia: Fortress, 1970.

Borg, M. J. *Jesus: Conflict, Holiness and Politics in the Teachings of Jesus.* SBEC 5: New York/Toronto: Mellen, 1984.

Branick, Vincent P. "Apocalyptic Paul?" *Catholic Biblical Quarterly 47:664-675* (October 1985): 664.

Brueggemann, Walter. *Theology of the Old Testament: Testimony, Dispute, Advocacy.* Minneapolis: Fortress Press, 1997.

Bultmann, R. "Geschichte und Eschatologie im Neuen Testament," *Glauben und Verstehen*, Vol. III. Tubingen: J. C. B. Mohr [Paul Siebeck], 1962.

________. *The Presence of Eternity.* New York: Harper and Brothers, 1957.

Collins, John J. "Introduction. Towards the Morphology of a Genre." *Semeia 14. Apocalypse: The Morphology of a Genre,* ed. J. Collins; Chico, CA: Scholars, 1979.

__________. *Daniel with an Introduction to Apocalyptic Literature*, The Forms of the Old Testament Literature, eds. Rolf Knierim and Gene M. Tucker, Vol.20. Grand Rapids, Michigan: William B. Eerdmans Publishing Company, 1984.

__________. *The Apocalyptic Imagination: An Introduction to Jewish Apocalyptic Literature.* Grand Rapids, Michigan: William B. Eerdmans Publishing Company, 1984.

Davies, W. D. *Paul and Rabbinic Judaism: Some Rabbinic Elements in Pauline Theology.* New York and Evanston: Harper and Row, Publishers, 1948.

Ferch, Arthur J. "The Two Aeons and The Messiah in Pseudo-Philo, 4Ezrea, and 2Baruch." *Andrews University Seminary Studies 15* (Autumn 1970): 135.

Fuller, Reginald H. "Jesus, Paul and Apocalyptic." *Anglican Theological Review 71* (Spring 1989): 137.

Green, Joel B. and Scot McKnight, eds. *Dictionary of Jesus and the Gospels.* Leicester, England: Inter - Varsity Press, 1992. S.v. "Apocalyptic Teaching," by T. J. Geddet.

Hanson, Paul D. *The Dawn of Apocalyptic: The Historical and Sociological Roots of Jewish Apocalyptic Eschatology.* Philadelphia: Fortress Press, 1975.

Hawthorne, Gerald F. and Ralph P. Martin, eds. *Dictionary of Paul and His Letters.* Leicester, England: Inter - Varsity Press, 1993. S.v. "Apocalypticism," by D. E. Aune.

__________. *Dictionary of Paul and His Letters.* Leicester, England: Inter - Varsity Press, 1993. S.v. "Apocalyptic," by D. C. Allison, Jr.

Hooker, Morna D. *The Gospel According to Saint Mark*, Black's New Testament Commentary, ed. Henry Chadwick. Peabody, Massachusetts: Hendrickson Publishers, 1991.

Keck, Leander E. "Paul and Apocalyptic Theology." *Interpretation: A Journal of Bible and Theology* 38 (July 1984): 234.

Koch, Klaus. *The Rediscovery of Apocalyptic.* SBT 2/22; Naperville, IL: Allenson, 1972.

Ladd, George E. "New Testament Apocalyptic." *Review and Expositor 78* (Spring 1981): 208.

Lindblom, J. "Gibt es eine Eschagologie bei den alttestamentlichen Propheten?" in *Studia Theologica*, 6 (1952).

Marshall, I. Haward. *Luke-Historian and Theologian.* London: The Paternoster Press, 1970.

Morris, L. *Apocalyptic.* Grand Rapids, MI: Eerdmans, 1972.

Murdock, William R. "History and Revelation in Jewish Apocalypticism," *Interpretation: A Journal of Bible and Theology* (April 1967): 176.

Procksch, O. *Theologie des Alten Testaments*, Gutersloh 1950.

Reid, George J. *Apocrypha*, translated by Douglas J. Potter, Dedicated to the Sacred Heart of Jesus Christ [database on-line]. From the Catholic Encyclopedia, copyright © 1913 by the Encyclopedia Press, Inc. Electronic version copyright © 1997 by New Advent, Inc, accessed 1 March.

Reinhardt, Karl. Herodotus Persergeschichte, in geistige Uberdieferung, hsg. v. E. Grassi, Berlin 1940.

Ross, James Robert. "Living Between Two Ages." in *Handbook of Biblical Prophecy*, eds. Carl E. Argmerding and W. Ward Gascque. Grand Rapids, Michigan: Baker Book House, 1978.

Rowley, H. H. *The Relevance of Apocalyptic*, 2nd edn. Henceforth cited as *Apocalyptic*, London and Redhill 1947.

Russell, D. S. *From Early Judaism to Early Church*. Philadelphia: Fortress Press, 1986.

__________. *Prophecy and the Apocalyptic Dream: Protest and Promise.* Peabody, MA: Hendrickson Publishers, Inc, 1994.

Sawyer, John F. A. *Prophecy and the Prophets of the Old Testament,* Publication of Oxford Bible Series, eds. P. R. Ackroyd and G. N. Stanton. Oxford: Oxford University Press, 1987.

Schmithals, W. *The Apocalyptic Movement. Introduction and Interpretation.* New York: Abingdom, 1975.

Vielhauer, P. "Introduction." in *New Testament Apocrypha*, eds. E Hennecke and W. Schneemelcher, vol.2. Great Britain: Lutterworth Press, 1965.

Vos, Geerhardus. *Biblical Theology: Old and New Testament.* Grand Rapids, Michigan: WM. B. Eerdmans Publishing company, 1948.

Von Rad, Gerhard. *Old Testament Theology.* Vol. 2. *The Theology of Israel's Prophetic Traditions.* New York: Harper and Row, Publishers, 1965.